Skill Transmission, Sport and Tacit Knowledge

T0383742

Teaching the skills necessary to play sport depends partly on transmitting knowledge verbally, yet non-verbal or tacit knowledge also has an important role. A coach may tell a young athlete to 'move more dynamically', but it is undoubtedly easier to demonstrate with the body itself how this should be done. Skills such as developing a 'feel for the water' cannot simply be transmitted verbally; they are embodied in the tacit knowledge acquired from practice, repetition and experience.

This is the first sociological study of the transmission of skills through tacit knowledge in sport. Drawing on philosophy, sociology and theories of embodiment, it presents original research gathered from qualitative empirical studies of young athletes. It discusses the concept of tacit knowledge in relation to motor skills transmission in a variety of sports, including athletics, swimming and judo, and examines the methodological possibilities of studying tacit knowledge, as well as its challenges and limitations.

This is fascinating reading for all those with an interest in the sociology of sport, theories of embodiment, or skill acquisition and transmission.

Honorata Jakubowska works as a professor in the Institute of Sociology at Adam Mickiewicz University in Poznań, Poland. Her main research areas are the sociology of the body and embodiment, the sociology of sport, and gender studies. She is the author of two award-winning monographs in Polish and the co-editor of the *Sociology of Sport Reader*, and she has written 60 articles and book chapters. She is the principal investigator of two research projects financed by the Polish National Science Centre.

Routledge Focus on Sport, Culture and Society

Routledge Focus on Sport, Culture and Society showcases the latest cutting-edge research in the sociology of sport and exercise. Concise in form (20,000–50,000 words) and published quickly (within three months), the books in this series represent an important channel through which authors can disseminate their research swiftly and make an impact on current debates. We welcome submissions on any topic within the socio-cultural study of sport and exercise, including but not limited to such subjects as gender, race, sexuality, disability, politics, the media, social theory, Olympic Studies and the ethics and philosophy of sport. The series aims to be theoretically informed, empirically grounded and international in reach, and will include a diversity of methodological approaches.

For a complete list of titles in this series, please visit www.routledge.com/sport/series/RFSCS

Available in This Series

Skill Transmission, Sport and Tacit Knowledge

A Sociological Perspective

Honorata Jakubowska

Routledge
Taylor & Francis Group

LONDON AND NEW YORK

First published 2017
by Routledge

2 Park Square, Milton Park, Abingdon, Oxfordshire OX14 4RN
52 Vanderbilt Avenue, New York, NY 10017

Routledge is an imprint of the Taylor and Francis Group, an informa business

First issued in paperback 2019

British Library Cataloguing-in-Publication Data
A catalogue record for this book is available from the British Library

Library of Congress Cataloging-in-Publication Data
A catalog record for this book has been requested

ISBN: 978-1-138-28192-9 (hbk)
ISBN: 978-0-367-34507-5 (pbk)

Typeset in Times New Roman
by Apex CoVantage, LLC

In memory of my Dad, who was always proud of me and my sister and believed that we can achieve anything

Contents

Figures

Tables

Introduction

Since the 1980s, a 'somatic' or 'corporeal turn' (Sheets-Johnstone 2009) has been observed in the social sciences related to the criticism of the Cartesian dichotomy between the mind and the body and the perception of individuals and their knowledge as being disembodied (Turner 1984; Csordas 1990; Shilling 1993). As a consequence, in the last few decades the number of studies focused on the body and embodiment has grown significantly. These studies can be divided into four categories: (1) social theories of the body, (2) 'histories' of the body, (3) analyses of bodily techniques and (4) studies of the embodied experience (Brown *et al.* 2011: 494). At the same time, and as noted by Parviainen and Aromaa (2015), representatives of the social sciences have become increasingly more interested in the body as a source of knowledge and as a tool for its acquisition. Notions such as 'embodied knowledge', 'bodily knowledge', 'body knowledge' or 'somatic knowledge' have been used to describe this 'new' kind of knowledge. The term 'embodied knowledge' is defined, among others, as 'knowledge incorporated not just by the material body but by a being comprising mind, body and environment' (Gieser 2008: 303); it can also refer to 'the product of bodily enculturation (Downey 2010: 23), developed in bodily practices and acquired through imitation' (Parviainen and Aromaa 2015: 2).

The body and embodied knowledge play a crucial role in the field of sport. However, paradoxically, as was pointed out by Hockey and Allen-Collinson (2007), social studies have ignored the body's 'fleshy' and 'carnal' nature for a long time. The common use of Foucauldian theory, although enriching the sociological analysis of sport, has resulted in the body being considered mainly through its visual representation, as an element of discourse or as a site of disciplinary practices (Hockey and Allen-Collinson 2007; Sparkes and Smith 2012). Since the beginning of the twenty-first century, beyond the continuation of studies using this theoretical approach, one can observe a growing number of studies focused on embodiment and embodied knowledge, which remain, nevertheless, marginalised in some areas, such as physical education analysis (Brown and Payne 2009).

Sports skills acquisition has been analysed by representatives of social sciences mainly from the phenomenological perspective. Initially, the majority of publications had a theoretical nature, but in the last few years, although theoretical considerations are still common, more empirical studies have been conducted (Allen-Collinson and Hockey 2001, 2011; Brown and Payne 2009; Martínková and Parry 2012; Standal and Engelsrud 2013). Regardless of the differences, all authors assume that skills are acquired through practice and experience, and their embodiment. Therefore, this perspective is focused rather on the incorporation of skills than on the process of teaching them. Transmission of sports skills has largely been studied in the physical sciences, such as physiology, biomechanics and psychology, but they have not gained much attention in either sociology or anthropology (Sánchez García and Spencer 2014: 188). This omission can be explained by the fact that the social sciences have for a long time favoured propositional knowledge, that is, knowledge that can be codified, verbalised and easily transmitted (Fentress and Wickham 1992: 3). In sociology, a reflection on knowledge and its creation has been strongly developed (different forms of the sociology of knowledge), but only a small role has been attributed to embodied or tacit knowledge. As a consequence, skills understood as ways of knowing have been ignored (Moe 2004; Samudra 2008).

Although the concept of 'embodied knowledge' has dominated social studies, this book's author proposes to analyse a process of skills transmission by using a different concept – that of 'tacit knowledge' (Polanyi 1966). It is perceived as more fruitful to study the ways of transferring and teaching skills and to analyse them from the coach's perspective. The concept of tacit knowledge is focused on the limits of verbal transfer of knowledge, that is, the questions of whether and to what extent knowledge can be articulated and shared. As such, it allows us to analyse the boundaries of verbal explanation and the ways in which one deals with that what one has to teach but cannot do so through words.

A scientific literature review reveals that the term 'tacit knowledge' is much more popular in philosophy, the cognitive sciences and management sciences than in sociology, although the sociology of science should be indicated as an exception (Gourlay 2002). This omission may be surprising, particularly since tacit knowledge is present in many areas of social life and plays a key role in daily activities. Therefore, it is necessary to emphasise its universality and meaning, stressing at the same time the little interest in this kind of knowledge in sociology. Likewise, the concept of tacit knowledge has been rarely used in the social analysis of sport. Usually, authors refer only to Polanyi's (1966) concept, although it has been critically reviewed (Janik 1988; Neuweg 2004; Collins 2010; Gascoigne and Thornton 2013). Moreover, even if this concept is used, it is not largely discussed but appears rather as a theoretical inspiration.

This book is based on a research project on skills transmission during sport training sessions with children and young people (10–14 years old) and was financed by the National Science Centre in Poland (NCN 2014/13/B/ HS6/01367) and its smaller, French part by the Foundation Maison de Sciences de l'Homme (international mobility DEA Programme). The project's methodology was based on three research methods: situated interviews with experts, apprenticeship and video-based observations with the use of GoPro cameras. Three sport disciplines were analysed: (1) athletics (running, throwing, jumping), (2) swimming and (3) judo. The selection criteria were: (1) type of skills required in the sport discipline, (2) different use(s) of the body, (3) relation towards the opponent's body and (4) space (indoor vs. outdoor) and (5) place of the sport activity. A total of 15 situated interviews, 15 researchers' training sessions and 24 video-based observations were conducted in the years 2015 and 2016 in the Greater Poland Voivodeship (Wielkopolska), which lies in the western part of Poland. Additionally, 15 video-based observations were conducted in Toulouse, France, in 2016.

The choice of sport as an adequate and fruitful research area to study tacit knowledge resulted from several reasons. One reason was the significance of the body, embodiment and non-verbalised forms of knowledge transmission in this field. Teaching someone how to run, swim, play football or fight is based partly on verbalised knowledge which is written in manuals or transferred verbally during training sessions; however, a significant part is taught through demonstration, body correction and so on. For example, a young athlete may hear his/her coach say, 'hit dynamically' or 'catch it tightly', but it is undoubtedly easier to show the athlete how a given action should be done. Sports training is also about acquiring abilities, such as a 'feel for the ball' or a 'feel for the water', which have their definitions but in everyday sports practice are nearly impossible to explain. Second, sports coaches can be perceived as experts (Dreyfus and Dreyfus 1980) of tacit knowledge transmission; that is, they are aware of both the possibilities and limitations of verbal transfer of this knowledge and must be able to articulate their knowledge ('knowing'), explain a performed movement and see its details and nuances (Carlgren 2007; Magill 2011). Third, coaches and athletes are accustomed to having to continuously analyse training sessions and competitions as well as to record them, which is of significant importance from the point of view of research methodology. Fourth, the performance of professional athletes, that is, the best of them, represents and is presented (e.g. in training videos) as the 'pure form' (Hughson and Inglis 2002: 3), that is, a perfect execution of movement.

The study conducted should be seen as a basis and inspiration for the book; however, the book's aims exceed the project's research questions, as the book's main objectives are (1) to present and discuss the concept of tacit knowledge with reference to motor skills transmission, (2) to examine the methodological possibilities of studying tacit knowledge, including their challenges and limitations, and (3) to present the process of transmission of tacit knowledge by paying particular attention to the limits of its verbalisation.

The book consists of five chapters. The first chapter starts with the notion of skill and how it is understood. Then the distinction between 'knowing how' and 'knowing that' and the problem of verbalisation of embodied knowledge are discussed. The second part of the chapter is devoted to Polanyi's concept of tacit knowledge and the revisions that have been made to it throughout the years. In the concluding part, the definition of tacit knowledge as used in the author's own research project is presented. In the second chapter, one can find the results of the subject literature review as divided into three categories: theoretical approach, studied sports disciplines and research methods. The third chapter has a methodological character. It presents the research project on which the book is based. The three main methods used in its framework are described: situated interviews with experts, apprenticeships and video-based observations with the use of GoPro cameras. The fourth chapter describes the process of sports skills transmission and the main teaching methods (verbal communication, demonstration, visual tools, imaginative methods, proxemics). The relations among these methods as well as the limits of verbal communication are the most important issues raised in this chapter. Chapter 4 also presents the practices used by coaches to make their demonstration more visible, such as reduction in speed and fragmentation. The final chapter is divided into two parts. In the first part, the question is posed regarding the possibility of exploring tacit knowledge; in the second part, the main challenges related to the possibility of writing about tacit knowledge are discussed.

Acknowledgements

I would like to thank the National Science Centre in Poland (project number: 2014/13/B/HS6/01367) and the Foundation Maison de Sciences de l'Homme in France (international mobility DEA Programme) for funding this research. The research project would not have been successful without all of the project's investigators, PhD students (Justyna Kramarczyk, Małgorzata Kubacka, Krzysztof Mączka, Ariel Modrzyk) and MA student (Ewelina Skoczylas). I would like to thank them for their participation and involvement in the project. I am also grateful to Professor Christine Mennesson, the director of the CRESCO laboratory at the University of Toulouse, and the laboratory's members (especially Lucie Forté-Gallois) for their help and warm reception in France. I would like to thank Simon Whitmore from

Routledge for giving me a chance to present the book's proposal. Another thanks goes to my sister, Agata Jakubowska, Professor at Adam Mickiewicz University, for her sisterly and scientific support. And last but not least, I would like to thank those people who believed and continue to believe in my scientific competences and support me in developing them.

References

Allen-Collinson, J. and Hockey, J., 2001, 'Runners' tales: Autoethnography, injury and narrative', *Auto/Biography*, 9(1–2), 95–106.
Allen-Collinson, J. and Hockey, J., 2011, 'Feeling the way: Notes towards a haptic phenomenology of distance running and scuba diving', *International Review for the Sociology of Sport*, 46, 330–345.
Brown, S.D., Cromby, J., Harper, D.J., Johnson, K. and Reavey, P., 2011, 'Researching "experience": Embodiment, methodology, process', *Theory and Psychology*, 21(4), 493–515.
Brown, T.D. and Payne, P.G., 2009, 'Conceptualizing the phenomenology of movement in physical education: Implications for pedagogical inquiry and development', *Quest*, 61, 418–441.
Carlgren, I., 2007, 'The content of schooling: From knowledge and subject matter to knowledge formation and subject specific ways of knowing', in E. Forsberg (ed.), *Curriculum Theory Revisited, Studies in Educational Policy and Educational Philosophy*, pp. 81–96, Uppsala University, Uppsala.
Collins, H.M., 2010, *Tacit and Explicit Knowledge*, University of Chicago Press, Chicago.
Csordas, T., 1990, 'Embodiment as a paradigm for anthropology', *Ethos*, 18, 5–47.
Downey, G., 2010, '"Practice without theory": A neuroanthropological perspective on embodied learning', *Journal of the Royal Anthropological Institute*, 16, 22–40.
Dreyfus, S. and Dreyfus, H., 1980, *A Five-Stage Model of the Mental Activities Involved in Directed Skill Acquisition*, University of California, Operations Research Centre, Berkeley.
Fentress, J. and Wickham, C., 1992, *Social Memory*, Blackwell, Oxford.
Gascoigne, N. and Thornton, T., 2013, *Tacit Knowledge*, Acumen, Durham.
Gieser, T., 2008, 'Embodiment, emotion and empathy: A phenomenological approach to apprenticeship learning', *Anthropological Theory*, 8, 299–318.
Gourlay, S., 2002, 'Tacit Knowledge, Tacit Knowing or Behaving', 3rd European Organizational Knowledge, Learning and Capabilities Conference, 5–6 April 2002, Athens, Greece. Viewed 23 September 2016 from http://eprints.kingston.ac.uk/2293/1/Gourlay%202002%20tacit%20knowledge.pdf.
Hockey, J. and Allen-Collinson, J., 2007, 'Grasping the phenomenology of sporting bodies', *International Review for the Sociology of Sport*, 42(2), 115–131.
Hughson, J. and Inglis, D., 2002, 'Inside the beautiful game: Towards a Merleau-Pontian phenomenology of soccer play', *Journal of the Philosophy of Sport*, 29, 1–15.

Janik, A., 1988, 'Tacit knowledge, working life and scientific method', in B. Göranzon and I. Josefson (eds.), *Knowledge, Skill and Artificial Intelligence*, pp. 53–63, Springer-Verlag, London.

Magill, R.A., 2011, *Motor Learning and Control: Concepts and Applications*, McGraw-Hill, New York.

Martínková, I. and Parry, J. (eds.), 2012, *Phenomenological Approach to Sport Studies*, Routledge, Abingdon, UK.

Moe, V.F., 2004, 'How to understand skill acquisition in sport', *Bulletin of Science, Technology and Society*, 24(3), 213–224.

Neuweg, G.H., 2004, 'Tacit knowing and implicit learning', in M. Fischer, N. Boreham and B. Nyham (eds.), *European Perspectives on Learning at Work: The Acquisition of Work Process Knowledge*, pp. 130–147, Office for Official Publications of the European Communities, Luxembourg.

Parviainen, J. and Aromaa, J., 2015, 'Bodily knowledge beyond motor skills and physical fitness: A phenomenological description of knowledge formation in physical training', *Sport, Education and Society*, DOI: 10.1080/13573322.2015.1054273.

Polanyi, M., 1966, *The Tacit Dimension*, University of Chicago Press, Chicago.

Samudra, J., 2008, 'Memory in our body: Thick participation and the translation of kinesthetic experience', *American Ethnologist*, 35, 665–681.

Sánchez García, R. and Spencer, D.C., 2014, 'Conclusion: Present and future lines of research', in R. García Sanchez and D.C. Spencer Dale (eds.), *Fighting Scholars: Habitus and Ethnographies of Martial Arts and Combat Sports*, pp. 185–191, Anthem Press, London and New York.

Sheets-Johnstone, M., 2009, *The Corporeal Turn: An Interdisciplinary Reader*, Imprint Academic, Exeter.

Shilling, C., 1993, *The Body and Social Theory*, SAGE Publications Ltd., London.

Sparkes, A. and Smith, B., 2012, 'Embodied research methodologies and seeking the senses in sport and physical culture: A fleshing out of problems and possibilities', *Qualitative Research on Sport and Physical Culture Research in the Sociology of Sport*, 6, 167–190.

Standal, Ø.F. and Engelsrud, G., 2013, 'Researching embodiment in movement contexts: A phenomenological approach', *Sport, Education and Society*, 18(2), 154–166.

Turner, B.S., 1984, *The Body and Society: Explorations in Social Theory*, Basil Blackwell, Oxford.

1 Embodied knowledge and the limits of its verbalisation

1.1 Knowing how

In this book, skills are perceived in terms of knowledge; the issue of whether they should be seen this way has already been discussed by several authors (Carr 1997; McNamee 1998; Parry 1998; Reid 1996; Parviainen 2002; Marchand 2008) and will thus be omitted. Despite the differences in understanding skills, they are usually described in a few features. First, they are learnt. Even if skills have, to some extent, a biological basis, they are developed through the process of learning, retention and transfer (Newell and Rosenbloom 1981). Second, as Guthrie (1952: 136) claimed, skills 'can be defined only in terms of success, of achievement, of a goal'. Third, skills development requires practice, and this is the only one way to become more successful; however, practice cannot guarantee success. Fourth, bodily skills are not completely separate from intellectual and cognitive skills; the term 'bodily' stresses that skills are manifested through body movements (Moe 2004: 214). And, finally, one can talk about the history of a skill's life and its development over time; that is, it is possible to indicate the beginning of its history, when somebody starts learning something, and its end, when the skill does not seem to improve anymore (Bernstein 1996; Bailey and Pickard 2010). As a consequence, it is quite easy to distinguish a novice from an expert.

Skills transfer and acquisition are realised through body practices, in and through the body (Marchand 2008). Thanks to training and experience, skills become incorporated (Leder 1990; Ingold 2000: 5). This process has been analysed by representatives of the social sciences mainly in the framework of the phenomenological approach (Kresse and Marchand 2009: 2) and by reference to the term 'embodied knowledge'. The theoretical concepts developed in the frame of this paradigm assume that knowledge is embodied, that knowing as a process is embodied and that the body is both the site and the 'subject' of knowing (Kupers 2008). Embodied knowledge is often described as corporeal knowhow, that is, the bodily *I can* (Standal and Engelsrud 2013), and skills are perceived as an element of 'knowing how' (Fraleigh 1987: 26). A distinction between 'knowing how' and 'knowing that' was introduced by Gilbert Ryle (1949). 'Knowing that' is 'propositional knowledge (theoretical or factual), since it conveys meaning, is based on rules or laws, and is not dependent on context' (Harris 2007: 3). The second kind of knowledge, 'knowing how', is understood as an ability, a complex of dispositions (Stanley and Williamson 2001: 411), the skill do to something; contrary to 'knowing that', 'knowing how' is 'situation-dependent, performative and non-propositional' (Harris 2007: 3).

Ryle's distinction has been discussed and questioned over the years by numerous authors (e.g. Stanley and Williamson 2001; Snowdon 2003; Bengson, Moffett and Wright 2009; Breivik 2014). The polemic has been focused on two main issues: (1) how are the two types of knowledge related, that is, are they indeed separate and (2) what does 'knowing-how' mean exactly? what does this knowledge consist of? (Fantl 2016). Some authors claim that 'knowing how' should not be perceived as distinctive from 'knowing that'. For example, according to Stanley and Williamson (2001), 'knowing how' is a species of 'knowledge that'. Moreover, the subject literature review provides several examples that contradict the understanding of 'knowledge how' as an ability to do something. One of these examples is that of an expert, such as a musician or a cook, who has lost his/her ability to perform a task because of body damage or illness (Stanley and Williamson 2001: 416; Snowdon 2003: 8). He/she knows how to play music or cook something but is not able to do so. In this context, Noë (2005) proposes to make a distinction between having the ability to do something and being able to do something. Another example refers to a person who has the ability do to something but does not have the knowledge as to how do it. For example, the expression 'beginner's luck' refers to a person has managed to do something very well although he/she does not have much knowledge about it.

Another issue that is discussed with reference to Ryle's dichotomy, and which is crucial from the perspective of this book, concerns the possibility of being able to verbalise both types of knowledge. Snowdon (2003: 27) stresses that 'the expression of knowledge ineliminably involves either gesture and or a response to the indication of samples'. By giving examples of sentences such as 'This fish which got away was THIS long' or 'The hat she was wearing was THAT shape, roughly', Snowdon reveals that knowledge can very often be expressible only in a specific context; therefore, even the 'knowledge that' is not always situation-independent. Moreover, there is knowledge based on sensory experiences and impressions which cannot be easily verbalised; therefore, 'knowing how' and 'knowing that' should not be perceived as a dichotomy, at least not on the basis of the possibility to verbalise it.

There has been a long academic debate on the difficulties in verbalising embodied knowledge in the fields of craft and the labour market (Harper 1987; O'Connor 2005; Marchand 2008; Sennett 2008), as well as in sport (Parviainen 2002; Crossley 2007; Samudra 2008). Douglas Harper (1987), in his analysis of a workshop, described 'working knowledge' as having to a large extent a bodily, non-verbalised nature. The author referred to two other concepts that are useful in the analysis of this kind of knowledge. The first is Levi-Strauss' (1969) bricoleur, that is, a person who uses resources (materials and objects) which are close at hand, who understands and makes use of the material world that surrounds him/her. The second type of knowledge is kinesthetic knowledge, which can be understood as the coordination of the hand, eye and mind. This knowledge refers to the various senses and allows one to evaluate a material through touch, to diagnose faults by hearing, and so on. As such, kinesthetic knowledge is difficult to transfer because it is difficult to articulate and express through words and notions. Richard Sennett, in his book titled *The Craftsman* concerning, among other topics, the acquisition of skills, noted that 'language struggles with depicting physical action, and nowhere is this struggle more evident than in language that tells us what to do' (Sennett 2008: 179).

Margaret Archer, the author of *Being Human: The Problem of Agency* (2000), indicated embodied knowledge as one of three types of knowledge. According to her, this kind of knowledge is 'know-how' knowledge and is based on the sensorimotor relation with nature. As such, it is almost or even completely non-verbalised. Two other kinds of knowledge were distinguished by Archer: discursive knowledge and practical knowledge. Regarding the latter, she argued that a large part of it cannot be easily expressed through words and that it relates to that part of reality which goes beyond the language.

The difficulty of transferring practical, embodied knowledge through words has also been emphasised in studies concerning sports skills. Jaida Kim Samudra (2008) has stressed this problem in the framework of the anthropological analysis which faces 'the peculiar difficulty of rendering into discourse exactly those practices his or her consultants consider verbally inexpressible' (p. 666). Using the example of *pencak silat* (Indonesian martial arts), she noted that in sport, movement is often perceived as a better medium of communication than verbal messages. Therefore, Samudra emphasised that something inexpressible should be not understood as non-communicative, as learners do communicate with one another; however, this communication has, to a large extent, a non-verbal character.

Gunn Nyberg (2014b), when exploring pole vaulters' 'knowing' noted that the possibility to articulate 'knowing how' is developed through practise. She perceived a coach as a person who should be able to articulate athletes' ways of moving, to communicate and reflect their actions. Nyberg also referred to Arnold's (1988) distinction between practical knowledge in the 'weak' and 'strong' sense: 'Knowing how to act, yet not knowing how the action was conducted' means a weak sense of practical knowledge, while 'being able to express and explain one's action represents a strong sense of practical knowledge' (Nyberg 2014b: 85).

Nick Crossley (2007) described a swimmer's knowledge as embodied knowledge, which is not discursive and 'cannot be put into discourse without distorting it' (p. 87). In Allan Janik's (1996) opinion, the knowledge of dancers and athletes remains tacit 'because there is no way to achieve it except by practising it' (p. 49). Jaana Parviainen, in her analysis of knowledge in dance, noticed that there is an articulated knowledge that is 'expressed in words, numbers, formulas, and procedures, communicated in an exact manner', but there is also bodily knowledge in dancing 'that cannot be articulated' (Parviainen 2002: 22). However, it is important to not perceive these kinds of knowledge as either competitive towards one another or isolated. On the contrary, they should be seen as interwoven and complementary in the process of knowledge transmission (Parviainen 2002; Kresse and Marchand 2009). Moreover, it would be incorrect to perceive verbalised knowledge as always comprehensive and situation-independent. In the process of skills acquisition, one can observe a significant number of verbalised messages that are understood only in a specific context. For example, during training sessions coaches use a large number of expressions that refer to the way of doing something or a part of the body whose movement should be changed that are situation-dependent (e.g. 'faster', 'head', 'legs'). This means of skills transmission refers to the example of how to ride a bike and the sentence 'That! is the way to ride!' as presented by Neil Gascoigne and Tim Thornton (2013: 169) in their book *Tacit Knowledge*. By using this case, among others, these authors explain their understanding of 'tacit knowledge', which has been chosen as a theoretical framework in the research project on which this book is based on.

1.2   Tacit knowledge

The concept of tacit knowledge was introduced by Michael Polanyi (1958, 1966). The term 'tacit' derives from the Latin adjective 'tacite', which is translated as 'without the use of speech', 'without express statement'. The verb 'taceo' means 'to be silent', 'to make no utterance', whereas the participle 'tacitus' means 'free of speech', 'not expressing itself through speech'.

These refer to the state of mind, behaviours, feelings and attitudes (Glare 1982: 1899–1900). In today's English, 'tacit' is defined as 'unspoken', 'implicit', 'understood or implied without being expressed directly' (Collins 2010: 4). The terms 'tacit' and 'implicit' are usually treated as antonyms of the word 'explicit', which means 'characterised by fully clear expression', 'clearly and fully developed or formulated' (Gove 1993: 801, 1135, 2326). However, in Polanyi's opinion, it is not easy to make a clear distinction between these two kinds of knowledge:

> While tacit knowledge can be possessed by itself, explicit knowledge must rely on being tacitly understood and applied. Hence, all knowledge is either tacit or rooted in tacit knowledge. A wholly explicit knowledge is unthinkable.
>
> (Polanyi 1969: 144)

Tacit knowledge is used in many activities in everyday life, such as being able to ride a bike, drive a car, play music or hammer a nail. Although one has the ability to do these kinds of activities, it is at the same time difficult to precisely define the essence of this 'know how' and to verbalise it. As Polanyi (1966: 4) states, 'we can know more than we can tell'.

His concept is based on two statements: the first, which will be discussed later, states that 'tacit knowledge is untellable'; the second is that it 'is personal knowledge, involving an "active comprehension of things known, an action that requires skill"' (Polanyi 1958: vii). This means that tacit knowledge should be seen as practical knowledge, related to skills and abilities which are developed through exercises and practice. 'Personal' also means that the process of knowledge acquisition passes through a single body and due to practice becomes an embodied basis for all other knowledge (Mitchell 2006: 63).

It is also important to note that Polanyi preferred to speak about 'knowing' than about 'knowledge'. By using the term 'knowing' he emphasised that acquisition of knowledge is a process (Polanyi 1969: 132; Nyberg 2014a). This term also allowed us, in his opinion, to overcome the distinction between theoretical and practical knowledge (Nyberg 2014b). He perceived understanding something and mastering a skill as nearly synonymous:

> Though we may prefer to speak of understanding a comprehensive object or situation and of mastering a skill, we do use the two words nearly as synonyms. Actually, we speak equally of grasping a subject or an art.
>
> (Polanyi 1969: 126)

Tacit knowing can also be perceived as the result of a process of knowledge acquisition, which Polanyi explains by using the example of car driving. At the beginning, a learning process is to a large extent based on verbalised instructions. Afterwards, the driver becomes more skilful, and his/her ability to drive is based on 'unspecifiable' knowledge which, due to training, undergoes automation and becomes difficult to verbalise. Therefore, knowing becomes tacit with time (Polanyi 1954: 382).

However, in the case of some skills, verbalisation can be difficult from the very beginning of the learning process, which is illustrated by Polanyi's famous example of learning how to ride a bike:

> We cannot learn to keep our balance on a bicycle by taking to heart that in order to compensate for a given angle of imbalance a, we must take a curve of the inside of the imbalance, of which the radius (r) should be proportionate to the square of the velocity (v) over the imbalance.
>
> (Polanyi 1969: 144)

Polanyi's concept has been discussed and reviewed by numerous authors, among them by Allan Janik (1988, 1990), Harry Collins (2010), Georg Hans Neuweg (2004), Neil Gascoigne and Tim Thornton (2013), and Frank Adloff, Katharina Gerund and David Kaldewey (2015). From this book's perspective, a crucial issue that has been discussed is that of the 'untellable' character of tacit knowledge, which is closely related to the question of whether tacit knowledge should be seen as opposite to explicit knowledge. Most authors do not agree that all tacit knowledge is 'untellable' and have proposed that different types of tacit knowledge be distinguished.

The basic distinction that appears in the literature assumes two main kinds of tacit knowledge: the first, called 'cognitive' tacit knowledge, refers to beliefs and mental models; the second, 'technical' tacit knowledge, which is the focus of this book, is related to motor skills and concrete know-how (Nonaka and Takeuchi 1995; Gourlay 2002). Allan Janik (1988) also recognised two kinds of knowledge when taking into account another criterion; namely, the first kind of tacit knowledge refers to things that can be verbalised, although they are not because a group of people does not want to share this knowledge or there was no need to put it into words. In the frame of this kind of knowledge, Janik distinguished among (1) trade and political secrets, (2) things overlooked and (3) presuppositions. The second kind of tacit knowledge refers to things that are by their nature incapable of being *precisely* articulated, that is, 'we know things without being able to put what we know into words' (p. 54). In this case, one can also speak about knowledge by acquaintance or familiarity. On the one hand, this knowledge refers to sensuous experience, while on the other hand to an 'open-textured character of rule-following behaviour', that is, knowledge acquired through repetition and practice.

Harry Collins (1974), in his earlier publications, stated that all knowledge consists partially of 'tacit rules which may be impossible to formulate' (p. 167). In his more recent publications he defined tacit knowledge as:

Knowledge or abilities that can be passed between scientists by personal contact but cannot be, or have not been, set out or passed on in formulae, diagrams, or verbal descriptions and instructions for action.

(Collins 2001: 72)

Collins distinguished three major kinds of tacit knowledge on the basis of three main reasons why this knowledge is not explicated: (1) relational, (2) somatic and (3) collective tacit knowledge. He named them as weak, medium and strong tacit knowledge, where the adjectives refer to 'the degree of resistance of the tacit knowledge to being explicit' (Collins 2010: 85). The relational (weak) tacit knowledge can be made explicit to the largest extent, and its tacit nature results from the character of human relations, tradition or logistic reason. In the framework of this kind of knowledge, Collins distinguished, among others, concealed knowledge, which can be deliberately kept hidden. As examples one can indicate the knowledge of experts and the knowledge of small groups that have their own non-verbal communication system. A second type of relational tacit knowledge is ostensive knowledge which 'is learned by pointing to some object or practice' (Collins 2010: 93) because its verbal description would be too complex, both to express and to understand. Collins also speaks about 'logistically demanding knowledge', which is similar to the 'working knowledge' described by Douglas Harper (1987). One can see this kind of knowledge while observing an experienced worker who is not always able to say where his/her tools are but can always find them; the last example of relational tacit knowledge is unrecognised knowledge.

The second type of tacit knowledge as distinguished by Collins and mentioned above is somatic (medium) tacit knowledge, which is the closest to Polanyi's perception of tacit knowledge. To describe it, Collins refers to Polanyi's examples of riding a bike and driving a car. This knowledge is related to the properties of individuals' bodies and brains and is expressed in habitual activities. Like other authors, including Polanyi himself, Collins (2010) emphasised that this kind of knowledge is not learnt due to written or verbalised instructions but is acquired during direct interactions:

We do not learn bicycle riding just from being told about it (coaching rules and second-order rules aside), or reading about it, but from demonstration, guided instruction, and personal contact with others who can ride – the modes of teaching associated with tacit knowledge.

(p. 99)

Both of these kinds of individual tacit knowledge are similar, to a large extent, to Janik's proposition. However, Collins (2010) also distinguished a third kind of tacit knowledge, that is collective (strong) tacit knowledge, which is related to the social community and 'the way society is constituted' (p. 85). It is acquired via interactions in the framework of a particular community, and it is not verbalised. Collins once again refers to the examples of riding a bike and driving a car, this time in different countries with different cultures of both riding and driving. Riding a bike will be perceived as acquired knowledge when one is able to ride a bike in street traffic among other bicycle riders, drivers and pedestrians. The same can be said about playing in a musical group and on a sports team. In all of these situations, knowledge becomes embodied through social practices.

Georg Hans Neuweg is another author who analysed the concept of tacit knowledge. According to Neuweg (2004), tacit knowing (1) concerns knowing understood as a process, (2) is focused on the 'relationship between knowing and its articulated counterpart', and (3) means that some human dispositions are 'unformalisable' and/or 'unteachable only by verbal instructions' (pp. 131–132). Neuweg noticed that the term 'tacit knowledge' is understood in scientific discourse via three different, although interrelated, meanings. First, it is understood as an ability to '[do] something intelligently in an intuitive manner'. The second meaning refers to Polanyi (1966) and Schön (1991); tacit knowing is understood here as 'the residue left unsaid by a detective articulation'. In this understanding, one can suppose that somebody is able to act skilfully but is not able to articulate what he/she knows or to articulate it appropriately. The third definition speaks about collective unconscious rules. Neuweg also distinguished three types of tacit knowledge:

1   tacit knowing-how – 'the tacit side of expertise that is more than, or different from, the application of theory' (e.g. the art of cooking)
2   tacit knowing-that – 'knowledge taken for granted'; based on a cognitive background, mental models or beliefs; difficult or impossible to describe
3   tacit roots of explicit knowledge, which refers to the assumption that all knowledge is fundamentally tacit.

(pp. 138–140)

According to Bengt Molander (1992), one can talk about tacit knowledge with reference to the knowledge that is transmitted through the exemplary actions of a master and is acquired through training and personal experience. Its core consists of the abilities to make judgements and to do things in practice. The author emphasised the body's role in tacit knowledge, which is illustrated by such skills as the *right movement* of the hand or having a *good eye*. The body is a tool of knowledge transmission, and theoretical knowledge must be incarnated to perform an activity skilfully. Molander, similar to Neuweg, also distinguished three main senses (or sides) of tacit knowledge. The first is knowledge that is not possible to describe or articulate in words, and the second is knowledge that is taken for granted. In relation to the first sense, Molander (1992) stated that it would be better to speak about the inexhaustibility of knowledge and in a wider context of reality, which means that 'no description and no presentation exhausts a particular body of professional knowledge' (p. 15). The third sense of tacit knowledge as distinguished by Molander (1992) is 'silenced' knowledge, which is understood as 'the knowledge of people who have not been given a voice or have not been allowed to use their own voice' (p. 16).

Frank Adloff *et al.* (2015) differentiated between two forms of tacit knowledge, 'weak' and 'strong', basing his division on the degree of knowledge accessibility and explicability. The former can be articulated explicitly, whereas the latter cannot be articulated but 'becomes visible and thus explicates itself in bodily acts' (Adloff *et al.* 2015: 13). However, in Adloff et al.'s opinion, access to 'pure' tacit knowledge ('one-to-one representation of tacit knowledge') is not possible because it is transformed when translated into explicit (verbalised) knowledge. Therefore, one should see the difference between knowing to do something and the explanation of how to do something.

Alexis Shotwell found the dichotomies between explicit and tacit and propositional and non-propositional knowledge 'inadequate' and proposed to use the umbrella term of 'implicit understanding':

> 'Implicit' here carries the meaning of something not (or not currently) expressed in words, whereas 'understanding' is meant to name an epistemic state in general may not achieve the status of knowledge traditionally defined.
>
> (Shotwell 2015: 172)

Shotwell indicated four, intertwined, as she emphasises, types of 'implicit understanding':

1 practical, skill-based or 'knowing-how' understanding – a kind of ability, a capacity to do something (e.g. swimming or playing a musical instrument), know-how developed through practice
2 socially situated habitus, which refers to Bourdieu's (1977) concept and means socially situated embodiment, incorporated expression of social norms

3   potentially propositional beliefs which remain tacit – commonsensical understanding, presuppositions, prejudices that can be put into words but are not

4   affective or emotional understanding – emotions and feeling, both common and inchoate, that are not easy to name.

(pp. 172–174)

Shotwell defined these types of understanding as 'unspeakable' or 'unspoken' and, as such, 'distinguishable from propositional knowledge' (p. 174). She stressed that propositional claims about some skills cannot be treated as a capacity do to something.

Neil Gascoigne and Tim Thornton (2013) also discussed Polanyi's statement that 'tacit knowledge is untellable' and noticed the following:

> It is untellable so far as the tellable is equated with what can be codified in general terms. In this respect, tacit knowledge contrast with explicit knowledge only in so far as the latter implies such context-free codification. (. . .) It can be articulated, then, but only practically and in context-dependent terms employing demonstrative concepts.

(p. 7)

According to Gascoigne and Thornton, tacit knowledge can be expressed verbally; however, it will be understood only in a particular situation as illustrated by the above-mentioned example of how to ride a bike and the sentence 'That! is the way to ride' (p. 63). The word 'that' is comprehensible only in a particular interaction and by its participants because 'tacit knowledge cannot be conveyed by situation-independent linguistic instruction' (Gascoigne and Thornton 2013: 169).

Gascoigne and Thornton criticised Ryle's distinction between 'knowledge that' and 'knowledge how' and, instead of this distinction, proposed to distinguish 'theoretical knowledge how' and 'practical knowledge how'. 'Theoretical knowledge how' means that one (theoretically) knows how to ride a bike, play tennis or play a music instrument. Answering the questions as to how to do it, a person uses, to a large extent, answers that are 'general and fully linguistically codified' (Gascoigne and Thornton 2013: 69). When starting sports trainings, one can possess 'theoretical knowledge how' from manuals, classes or video films, but that knowledge is not automatically transferred into 'practical knowledge how', that is, being able to ride a bike, play tennis, and so forth.

'Theoretical knowledge how' is context-independent, whereas 'practical knowledge how' is context-dependent; therefore one can observe the differences in their transfer, which Gascoigne and Thornton (2013: 188) explained by using the tennis example. Tennis shots have names; therefore, if a learner knows the names, it will be sufficient for the coach to ask a tennis player to use a particular shot. A coach can also make a demonstration him/herself or show another player who is using the shot. Both ways of explanation used in the right context are connected with the transfer of theoretical knowledge of how to play. They can also be perceived as the transfer of practical knowledge in the case of a skilled player 'with an armoury of practical knowledge of shots', a player who knows not only the name of a shot but also has knowledge of how to execute it. For a less-skilled player, the coach will demonstrate a shot; the novice will need a large amount of practice and the coach's feedback to acquire this practical knowledge how.

Although tacit knowledge cannot always be verbalised, it can be shared and transmitted (Gascoigne and Thornton 2013). Polanyi indicated three main mechanisms of tacit knowledge transmission: imitation, identification and learning-by-doing (Parviainen 2002: 21). This knowledge is the result of training in the direct relation between a master and a neophyte, between an experienced expert and a novice:

> By watching the master and emulating his efforts in the presence of his example, the apprentice unconsciously picks up the rules of the art, including those which are not explicitly known to the master himself.
>
> (Polanyi 1958: 53)

The process of transmission is based, to a large extent, on practical demonstration and practical exercises. This does not mean that verbal instructions are absent from this process; however, they rarely occur alone. Moreover, verbalised knowledge can usually be understood only in a particular situation, when it is articulated. Therefore, the process of skills' transmission requires not only a direct relation between the master and the neophyte, but also a specific context and a particular place, such as a sports venue.

The concept of 'tacit knowledge' has not been largely used in previous social studies concerning transfer and acquisition of embodied sports skills. An exception are Gunn Nyberg's publications, such as her doctoral thesis 'Ways of knowing in ways of moving. A study of the meaning of capability' (Nyberg 2014a). In this thesis, Nyberg referred to Polanyi (1966) and Janik's (1996) considerations of tacit knowledge. Nyberg also used Polanyi's concept of tacit knowledge in her other publications, both theoretical and empirical (Nyberg 2014b, 2015; Nyberg and Larsson 2014). One of her studies revealed that freeskiers' knowing has both a theoretical and a practical dimension, which is partly tacit; however it is possible to articulate to a certain extent (Nyberg 2015). Nyberg (2014b) also used Polanyi's concept as well as those of Ryle (1949) and Schön (1991) in her article on the practical knowledge of pole vaulters. Taking this elite sport as an example, she stated that the exploration of 'knowing in movement' can develop movement education in physical education.

In her articles, Nyberg (2014b, 2015) has emphasised the difficulty of trying to articulate movement knowing, 'knowledge in use' (Neuweg 2004: 131), and, as a consequence, chose as her informants experienced athletes and coaches. They are perceived as 'the experts', which means not only that they have reached an expert level (Dreyfus and Dreyfus 1980), but also, and more important from the methodological point of view, that they are able to articulate their knowing and explicate what they are doing when performing movements (Carlgren 2007; Magill 2011).

Besides Nyberg's publications, the term 'tacit knowledge' has appeared very rarely with reference to the sports field, and it is nearly absent in social science studies of the subject. As the exceptions, one can indicate Lin Ma's (2015) theoretical paper focused on understanding tacit knowledge and its role in sports teaching. Ma stated that 'in sports teaching, the teacher should be tacit with students to form effective interaction of tacit knowledge', and she distinguished two transmission modes of tacit knowledge: 'apprenticeship' and 'explicit'. Lisa Schindler (2009) refers to Polanyi's concept in her interesting publication on 'vis-ability' with reference to the analysis of video data. The results of her study will be discussed together with my own study results. In Neil Stephens and Sara Delamont's (2009) paper on capoeira, the term 'tacit knowledge' appeared to describe *malicia* as an example of tacit, indeterminate skills. As the theoretical framework, the authors used the distinction proposed by Jamous and Peloille (1970) 'separating the indeterminate or tacit from the technical skills and knowledge, which are explicit and even codified' (Stephens and Delamont 2009: 537), as well as the concept of habitus (Bourdieu 1977).

As this chapter shows, tacit knowledge has been discussed by several authors who proposed similar, but not identical, understandings of the concept and distinguished different kinds of tacit knowledge. On the basis of these theoretical considerations, a definition of tacit knowledge has been created for the purpose of this book and this author's research project. It is understood as individual knowledge which is embodied and refers to motor (sports) skills and exists in sports skills. This tacit knowledge can be verbalised, although not completely; however, its understanding is situation-dependent. Tacit knowledge is transferred to a large extent through demonstration and other forms of non-verbal communication and acquired by imitation and practice. As such, it questions the dichotomy between comprehensible and accessible verbalised knowledge and inaccessible, untellable knowledge.

References

Adloff, F., Gerund, K. and Kaldewey, D. (eds.), 2015, *Revealing Tacit Knowledge: Embodiment and Explication*, transcript Verlag, Bielefeld.

Archer, M., 2000, *Being Human: The Problem of Agency*, Cambridge University Press, Cambridge.

Arnold, P.J., 1988, 'Education, movement, and the rationality of practical knowledge', *Quest*, 40(2), 115–125.

Bailey, R. and Pickard, A., 2010, 'Body learning: Examining the processes of skill learning in dance', *Sport, Education and Society*, 15(3), 367–382.

Bengson, J, Moffett, M.A. and Wright, J.C., 2009, 'The folk on knowing how', *Philosophical Studies*, 142(3), 387–401.

Bernstein, N., 1996, 'On dexterity and its development', in M. Latash and M. Turvey (eds.), *Dexterity and Its Development*, pp. 3–244, Lawrence Erlbaum Associates, Mahwah, NJ.

Bourdieu, P., 1977, *Outline of a Theory of Practice*, Cambridge University Press, Cambridge.

Breivik, G., 2014, 'Sporting knowledge and the problem of knowing how', *Journal of the Philosophy of Sport*, 41(2), 143–162.

Carlgren, I., 2007, 'The content of schooling: From knowledge and subject matter to knowledge formation and subject specific ways of knowing', in E. Forsberg (ed.), *Curriculum Theory Revisited, Studies in Educational Policy and Educational Philosophy*, pp. 81–96, Uppsala University, Uppsala.

Carr, D., 1997, 'Physical education and value diversity: A response to Andrew Reid', *European Physical Education Review*, 3(2), 1995–2005.

Collins, H.M., 1974, 'The TEA set: Tacit knowledge and scientific networks', *Science Studies*, 4(2), 165–185.

Collins, H.M., 2001, 'What is tacit knowledge?', in T.R. Schatzki, K. Knorr Cetina and E. von Savigny (eds.), *The Practice Turn in Contemporary Theory*, pp. 107–119, Routledge, Abingdon, UK.

Collins, H.M., 2010, *Tacit and Explicit Knowledge*, University of Chicago Press, Chicago.

Crossley, N., 2007, 'Researching embodiment by way of "body techniques"', *The Sociological Review*, 55(1), 80–94.

Dreyfus, S. and Dreyfus, H., 1980, *A Five-Stage Model of the Mental Activities Involved in Directed Skill Acquisition*, University of California, Operations Research Centre, Berkeley.

Fantl, J., 2016, 'Knowledge how', in E.N. Zalta (ed.), *The Stanford Encyclopedia of Philosophy* (Spring 2016 ed.). Viewed 7 November 2016 from https://plato.stanford.edu/archives/spr2016/entries/knowledge-how/

Fraleigh, S., 1987, *Dance and the Lived Body*, University of Pittsburgh Press, Pittsburgh.

Gascoigne, N. and Thornton, T., 2013, *Tacit Knowledge*, Acumen, Durham.

Glare, P. (ed.), 1982, *Oxford Latin Dictionary*, Clarendon Press, Oxford.

Gourlay, S., 2002, 'Tacit Knowledge, Tacit Knowing or Behaving', 3rd European Organizational Knowledge, Learning and Capabilities Conference, 5–6 April 2002, Athens, Greece. Viewed 23 September 2016 from http://eprints.kingston. ac.uk/2293/1/Gourlay%202002%20tacit%20knowledge.pdf

Gove, P. (ed.), 1993, *Webster's Third New International Dictionary of the English Language*, Merriam-Webster, Springfield.

Guthrie, E., 1952, *The Psychology of Learning*, Harper and Brothers, New York.

Harper, D., 1987, *Working Knowledge: Skill and Community in a Small Shop*, University of Chicago Press, Chicago.

Harris, M. (ed.), 2007, *Ways of Knowing: Anthropological Approaches to Crafting Experience and Knowledge*, Berghahn, New York.

Ingold, T., 2000, *The Perception of the Environment: Essays on Livelihood, Dwelling and Skill*, Routledge, London.

Jamous, H. and Peloille, B., 1970, 'Professions or self-perpetuating systems?', in J.A. Jackson (ed.), *Professions and Professionalization*, pp. 115–152, Cambridge University Press, Cambridge.

Janik, A., 1988, 'Tacit knowledge, working life and scientific method', in B. Göranzon and I. Josefson (eds.), *Knowledge, Skill and Artificial Intelligence*, pp. 53–63, Springer-Verlag, London.

Janik, A., 1990, 'Tacit knowledge, rule-following and learing', in B. Göranzon and M. Florin (eds.), *Artificial Intelligence, Culture and Language: On Education and Work*, pp. 45–55, Springer, London.

Janik, A., 1996, *Kunskapsbegrepp i praktisk filosofi* [*Concept of Knowledge in Philosophy of Practice*], Brutus Östlings Bokförlag Symposion, Skåne län.

Kresse, K. and Marchand, T.H.J., 2009, 'Introduction: Knowing in practice', *Africa*, 79(1), 1–16.

Kupers, W., 2008, 'Knowing in organizations: Pheno-practical perspectives', in P. Ordonez de Pablos, R. Tennyson and M.D. Lytras (eds.), *Knowledge Networks: The Social Software Perspective*, pp. 131–150, IGI Global, Hershey, PA.

Leder, D., 1990, *The Absent Body*, University of Chicago Press, Chicago.

Levi-Strauss, C., 1969, *The Elementary Structures of Kinship*, Beacon Press, Boston.

Ma, L., 2015, 'Analysis on Existence and Transmission of Tacit Knowledge in Sports Teaching', The International Conference on Education Technology and Economic Management, 14–15 March 2015, Beijing. Viewed 23 September 2016 from http://www.atlantis-press.com/php/pub.php?publication=icetem-15&frame=http%3A//www.atlantis-press.com/php/paper-details.php%3Fid%3D16610

Magill, R.A., 2011, *Motor Learning and Control: Concepts and Applications*, McGraw-Hill, New York.

Marchand, T.H.J., 2008, 'Muscles, moral and mind: Craft apprenticeship and the formation of person', *British Journal of Educational Studies*, 56(3), 245–271.

McNamee, M., 1998, 'Philosophy and physical education: Analysis, epistemology and axiology', *European Physical Education Review*, 4, 75–91.

Mitchell, M.T., 2006, *Michael Polanyi*, ISI Books, Wilmington.

Moe, V.F., 2004, 'How to understand skill acquisition in sport', *Bulletin of Science, Technology and Society*, 24(3), 213–224.

Molander, B., 1992, 'Tacit knowledge and silenced knowledge: Fundamental problems and controversies', in B. Göranzon and M. Florin (eds.), *Skill and Education: Reflection and Experience*, pp. 9–31, Springer-Verlag, London.

Neuweg, G.H., 2004, 'Tacit knowing and implicit learning', in M. Fischer, N. Boreham and B. Nyham (eds.), *European Perspectives on Learning at Work: The Acquisition of Work Process Knowledge*, pp. 130–147, Office for Official Publications of the European Communities, Luxembourg.

Newell, A. and Rosenbloom, P.S., 1981, 'Mechanisms of skill acquisition and the law of practice', in J.R. Anderson (ed.), *Cognitive Skills and Their Acquisition*, pp. 1–55, Erlbaum, Hillsdale, NJ.

Noë, A., 2005, 'Against intellectualism', *Analysis*, 65(4), 278–290.

Nonaka, I. and Takeuchi, H., 1995, *The Knowledge-Creating Company: How Japanese Companies Create the Dynamics of Innovation*, Oxford University Press, New York.

Nyberg, G., 2014a, *Ways of Knowing in Ways of Moving: A Study of the Meaning of Capability to Move*, Stockholm University, Stockholm.

Nyberg, G., 2014b, 'Exploring "knowings" in human movement: The practical knowledge of pole-vaulters', *European Physical Education Review*, 20(1), 72–89.

Nyberg, G., 2015, 'Developing a "somatic velocimeter": The practical knowledge of freeskiers', *Qualitative Research in Sport, Exercise and Health*, 7(1), 109–124.

Nyberg, G. and Larsson, H., 2014, 'Exploring "what" to learn in physical education', *Physical Education and Sport Pedagogy*, 19(2), 123–135.

O'Connor, E., 2005, 'Embodied knowledge: The experience of meaning and the struggle towards proficiency in glassblowing', *Ethnography*, 6(2), 183–204.

Parry, J., 1998, 'Reid on knowledge and justification in physical education', *European Physical Education Review*, 4(1), 70–74.

Parviainen, J., 2002, 'Bodily knowledge: Epistemological reflections on dance', *Dance Research Journal*, 34(1), 11–26.

Polanyi, M., 1954, 'Skills and connoisseurship', in *Atti del congresso di studi metodologici*, pp. 381–394, Edizioni Ramella, Torino.

Polanyi, M., 1958, *Personal Knowledge*, University of Chicago Press, Chicago.

Polanyi, M., 1966, *The Tacit Dimension*, University of Chicago Press, Chicago.

Polanyi, M., 1969, *Knowing and Being: Essays by Michael Polanyi*, The University of Chicago Press, Chicago.

Reid, A., 1996, 'Knowledge, practice and theory in physical education', *European Physical Education Review*, 2(2), 94–104.

Ryle, G., 1949, *The Concept of Mind*, London: Routledge.

Samudra, J., 2008, 'Memory in our body: Thick participation and the translation of kinesthetic experience', *American Ethnologist*, 35, 665–681.

Schindler, L., 2009, 'The production of <<vis-ability>>: An ethnographic video analysis of a martial arts class', in U. Kissmann (ed.), *Video Interaction Analysis: Methods and Methodology*, pp. 135–154, Peter Lang, Frankfurt am Main.

Schön, D.A., 1991, *The Reflective Practitioner: How Professionals Think in Action*, Basic Books, London.

Sennett, R., 2008, *The Craftsman*, Penguin Books, London.

Shotwell, A., 2015, 'Racial formation, implicit understanding, and problems with implicit association tests', in F. Adloff, K. Gerund and D. Kaldewey (eds.), *Revealing Tacit Knowledge: Embodiment and Explication*, pp. 169–184, transcript Verlag, Bielefeld.

Snowdon, P., 2003, 'Knowing how and knowing that: A distinction reconsidered', *Proceedings of the Aristotelian Society*, 104(1), 1–29.

Standal, Ø.F. and Engelsrud, G., 2013, 'Researching embodiment in movement contexts: A phenomenological approach', *Sport, Education and Society*, 18(2), 154–166.

Stanley, J. and Williamson, T., 2001, 'Knowing how', *The Journal of Philosophy*, 98(8), 411–444.

Stephens, N. and Delamont, S., 2009, '"They start to get malicia": Teaching tacit and technical knowledge', *British Journal of Sociology of Education*, 30(5), 537–548.

2 Exploring the process of embodied sports knowledge transmission – state of the art

2.1 Dominant theoretical framework

The aim of this chapter is to present a scientific literature review of the previous sociological as well as ethnographic, anthropological and philosophical publications and studies on the transmission of embodied sports knowledge. This review cannot be comprehensive due to the limits of this book's length; however, it presents the most often cited authors in the research field as well as authors whose publications have been important and inspiring for the author's own study. It should also be noted that the review is limited to articles and books published in English and, to a smaller extent, in French. The author is aware of the rich German literature related to the book's subject; however, she does not know German and could take into account only those publications that were written in English. The chapter presents the main theoretical perspectives that have been taken into account, the fields of analysis and the research methods that have been used. Finally, the author's own research project is positioned in reference to the existing scientific publications.

The concept of embodied (bodily) knowledge has usually been used by representatives of the social sciences to analyse a process of skills transfer and acquisition. Jaana Parviainen and Johanna Aromaa (2015: 2–3) distinguish three main directions in the recent sociological reflection on bodily knowledge. The first approach is based on post-structural theory and is widely used in the analysis of physical education (PE) (see, e.g. Fisette 2011; Ivinson 2012; Larsson and Quennerstedt 2012; Evans, Davies and Rich 2014). The second, pragmatic approach, which is the closest to the concept of tacit knowledge, emphasises practical knowledge, motor skills and embodied learning. In the framework of this approach, authors (Andersson, Östman and Öhman 2013; Breivik 2014; Ávila da Costa, McNamee and Lacerda 2014; Nyberg 2014a), by studying the process of sports skills' learning and its embodiment, refer, among others, to Ryle (1949) and Polanyi (1966) and their notions of practical and tacit knowledge, as well as to the concept of 'body techniques' as proposed by Mauss (1973[1935]). The third approach is a phenomenological one and is focused on knowledge incorporation and the body as a source of knowledge. The phenomenological approach is based on Merleau-Ponty's (2002[1945]) perception of embodiment. Two of Merleau-Ponty's concepts have influenced studies on embodiment knowledge, namely 'habit' and 'body schema'. Habit is understood as

> knowledge in the hands, which is forthcoming only when bodily effort is made, and cannot be formulated in detachment from that effort. The subject knows where the letters are on the typewriter as we know where one of our limbs is, through a knowledge bred of familiarity.
>
> (Merleau-Ponty 2002: 166)

This means that knowledge is expressed through the body. An embodied individual can do something and this ability (*I can*) is prior to *I know* (Standal and Engelsrud 2013: 157). A habit 'involves a modification and enlargement of the corporeal schema, an incorporation of new "principles" of action and know-how' (Crossley 2001: 125).

The corporeal (or body) schema itself is described by Nick Crossley (2001: 123) as 'an incorporated bodily know-how and practical sense; a perspectival grasp upon the world from the "point of view" of the body'. Thanks to the body schema, one 'knows without knowing' how to swim or ride a bike. The body schema is distinct from body image, which refers to intentional states, dispositions and attitudes. The body schema should be perceived as the body in action, while the body image represents the body and parts of the body's objectification. A body schema is transferred by intercorporeal learning, that is, observation and relations with other embodied learners, which are more fruitful than verbal communication (Standal and Engelsrud 2013: 158).

The concept of intercorporeal learning has been used and developed by several authors (Casey 1998; Sheets-Johnstone 2000; Jespersen 2003) who indicated observation and imitation as a basis of this kind of learning. As noted by Sheets-Johnstone:

> Skill-learning is rooted in the capacity *of one bodily presence to be attentive to another and to pattern movement along the lines of the other*, imitating the way in which the other performs something . . . imitation is not senseless copying but consistently engenders the possibility of deviating from and innovating common practice.
>
> (Sheets-Johnstone 2000: 358–359.
> Italics in the original version)

The phenomenological approach has dominated studies on skills acquisition. It is visible mainly in the analysis of craft apprenticeships (Coy 1989;

Dilley 1989; Marchand 2001; Herzfeld 2004; O'Connor 2005; Simpson 2006), which remain on the margins of this book, as well as in sports skills' analysis. The usefulness and implication of phenomenology in sports studies have been discussed in a book titled *Phenomenological Approach to Sport Studies*, edited by Irena Martínková and Jim Parry (2012), as well as in the work of several other authors (Kerry and Armour 2000; Hockey 2006; Hockey and Allen-Collinson 2007; Breivik 2008; Allen-Collinson 2009; Brown and Payne 2009; Allen-Collinson and Hockey 2011; Hogeveen 2011; Standal and Engelsrud 2013).

Publications by Greg Downey, whose research on capoeira has made an important contribution to the social studies of embodied sports skills, also fits into the phenomenological paradigm. His book titled *Learning Capoeira: Lessons in Cunning from an Afro-Brazilian Art* (Downey 2005a) is based on ethnography and is focused on the bodily sensations and skills in a learning process during which the masters train the novices. Capoeira has also been the topic of this author's other publications, in which he analysed the role of imitation in skills acquisition (Downey 2005b, 2007, 2008) and proposed to study embodied learning from a neuroanthropological perspective (Downey 2010). Capoeira has also been analysed by other authors, such as Sara Delamont and Neil Stephens (2006, 2008, 2009). The publications of these authors are methodologically interesting because they present a dual autoethnography which takes into account 'two authors, two voices, two embodied experiences, and two sociological biographies in dialogue' (Stephens and Delamont 2006: 316).

Apart from Merleau-Ponty, the works of two other authors have influenced the social analysis of bodily skills acquisition in the social sciences: Marcel Mauss and his concept of 'body techniques', and Pierre Bourdieu and his concept of 'habitus' (Kresse and Marchand 2009: 2), both of which are related to embodied learning.

Mauss defined body techniques as 'ways in which from society to society men know how to use their bodies' (1973[1935]: 70). Thus they are a form of knowledge, of embodied practical skills. Transmission of body techniques proceeds through apprenticeship, where observation and imitation are crucial:

> The individual borrows the series of movements which constitute [the bodily skill] from the action executed in front of him.
>
> (Mauss 1973[1935]: 73)

According to Crossley (2001), the concept of 'body techniques' allows one to study embodied knowledge and 'translates "embodiment" into a researchable format' (p. 87). This knowledge can be analysed and understood only in the form of embodied and practical competences, that is, body techniques, which Crossley illustrated by using the example of a swimmer's knowledge.

The concept of 'body techniques' as well as 'reflexive body techniques' as proposed by Crossley (2005) have been used in studies of martial arts and combat sports (Spencer 2009; Sánchez García and Spencer 2014; Graham 2014) and sailing (Andersson *et al.* 2013). Crossley (2005) defined 'reflexive body techniques' (RBTs) as 'those body techniques whose primary purpose is to work back upon the body, so as to modify, maintain or thematise it in some way' (p. 9). RBTs are reproduced by interactions with other embodied agents. On the one hand, these techniques are based on embodied knowledge, competencies and performed by the body and on the other, they modify the body to make it useful for specific purposes (Crossley 2004a, 2004b, 2005).

Dale C. Spencer, another important author in social studies on martial arts, refers in his studies to the phenomenological conception of habitus as well as to that of reflexive body techniques. On the basis of in-depth interviews and participant observation, Spencer analysed, for example, the production of a mixed martial arts (MMA) fighter habitus, that is, how MMA fighters engage in body callusing through the use of reflexive body techniques (Spencer 2009, 2011, 2012).

Representatives of the social sciences, and mainly those who have studied combat sports and martial arts, very often refer to the concept of 'habitus'. Dale C. Spencer and Raúl Sánchez García, editors of the book *Fighting Scholars: Habitus and Ethnographies of Martial Arts and Combat Sports*, noted in the introduction that habitus is 'conceptually paramount, as it opens the gates to the premises and perils of what Wacquant calls "carnal sociology"' (Sánchez García and Spencer 2014: 1).

This term was already used by Mauss (1973[1935]) to emphasise that the ways of using the body vary not only individually but also between societies, fashions and types of prestige. Nowadays, sociologists refer mainly to Bourdieu and his understanding of habitus as a set of embodied dispositions (tastes, thoughts, feelings, body postures) that are socially and culturally reproduced, that is, depend on social stratification (Bourdieu 1977).

In sports studies, the concept of habitus has become widespread by Loïc Wacquant and his book *Body and Soul: Ethnographic Notebooks of an Apprentice-Boxer* (2004) based on observant participation. Wacquant already referred to the concept of habitus in his previous publications when he described life and labour in the boxing gym (Wacquant 1989) and started to describe a process during which 'bodily capital' is moulded into 'pugilistic capital' (Wacquant 1995). This process occurs, as the author states, through embodied social practices and takes into account three elements: the flesh-and-blood body, the consciousness and the collectivity of the club (Wacquant 2004).

Wacquant (2004) understands habitus as 'a set of bodily and mental schemata' which is acquired via 'a largely implicit and barely codified pedagogy' (p. 16). He indicated four proprieties of habitus which emphasise its social nature: (1) it is a set of acquired dispositions, (2) this set of dispositions varies by social location and trajectory, (3) it operates beneath the level of consciousness and discourse, and (4) due to pedagogical work, the socially constituted conative and cognitive structures of habitus are malleable and transmissible (Wacquant 2011).

For Wacquant (2011), habitus is both a research topic and a tool. In the first case, it becomes a topic of investigation, and the process if its acquisition is analysed. In the second case, its possession simplifies access to a particular sports field and allows one to explore from and with the body. This understanding of habitus, as well as the methodology chosen by Wacquant (observant participation), has allowed, in Sánchez García and Spencer's opinion, a rejection of a false dichotomy between distant observation and 'going native', instead of which:

> we 'go native but armed' with the theory of habitus in order to capture the production of the skilled, sensitive and desiring body by undergoing the process studied.
>
> (Sánchez García and Spencer 2014: 5)

The focus on embodiment and embodied practices has generated interest in the role of the different senses that influence understanding and awareness of the body (Sparkes 2009, 2010, 2016). One cannot be surprised that researchers have drawn their attention to the role of the senses in sports practices since

> sports participants hear, smell, see, touch and move within their particular sporting environments, whether hockey pitch, mountain face, ice rink or squash court.
>
> (Hockey and Allen-Collinson 2007: 123)

An athlete hears when he/she properly hits a rocket, 'feels' the ball, strikes a competitor in a certain way, and so on. The sensual dimension of experiences in the field of sports has been revealed by Wacquant (2004) and Downey (2005a), and in recent years it has been described by a number of authors as the result of their autoethnographic studies (Hockey 2006; Sparkes 2009, 2010; Allen-Collinson and Hockey 2011; Merchant 2011), during which the researcher's body became the main 'instrument' of sensual data collection (Sparkes 2016: 46). In this way, sports analysis fits into wider interest in the senses and sensory or multi-sensory knowledge and the rising meaning of sensory ethnography (Brown, Dilley and Marshall 2008; Pink 2009). One of the main challenges that researchers face in studying the different senses is the issue of their verbalisation, that is, the transmission of senses into appropriate words. Although this problem is limited in the case of sight (due to this sense's domination in our culture), it does occur in reference to the other senses, such as hearing and smelling. In this meaning, knowledge based on sensual experience can be perceived, as was proposed by Janik (1988), as a type of tacit knowledge.

2.2   Studied sports disciplines

As the previous examples showed, boxing, capoeira and mixed martial arts have largely been analysed in social research. *Pencak silat* (*silek*) is another martial art which has been the object of social investigations, as illustrated by the publications of Jean-Marc de Grave (2001, 2011), Douglas Farrer (2007) and Jaida Kim Samudra (2008); Samudra stressed the meaning of the researcher's embodied participation in the conducted study. One can also find other publications on boxing (Mennesson 2000, 2004; Matthews D. 2002; Oualhaci 2014; Matthews Ch. 2015) and other martial arts, such as taekwondo (Graham 2014) and judo (Law 2008).

Embodied knowledge in martial arts has also been analysed by contributors to the book *Martial Arts as Embodied Knowledge*, edited by D. S. Farrer and John Whalen-Bridge (2011). The collection is focused on forms of knowledge characterised as 'being-in-the-world' (Merleau-Ponty 2002) and embodied practices. Embodiment itself is understood by the editors 'both as an ineluctable fact of martial training, and as a methodological cue' (Farrer and Whalen-Bridge 2011: 1). Similar to the above-mentioned publications, the majority of chapters in *Martial Arts as Embodied Knowledge* were written by scholars-learners. The essays, as noted by the editors, are focused on the practices rather than on being a critical literature review.

Martial arts and combat sports have been the most-often analysed sports disciplines in the framework of social research on embodied knowledge in sport. According to Sánchez García and Spencer (2014), these sports disciplines 'are perspicuous settings to study and develop the project of a carnal sociology with "habitus", "body techniques" and "technologies of the self" as key points of research' (pp. 1–2). The authors also indicated three main reasons why the social sciences will benefit from studies on martial arts and combat sports. The first is the possibility to observe the management of violence, also in the context of gender relations and their reproduction. It should be noted that although a majority of studies in the field of martial arts and combat sports have been conducted by male researchers, one can observe a growing number of female authors in this field (e.g. Mennesson

2000, 2004; Guérandel and Mennesson 2007; Samudra 2008; Schindler 2009; Schneider 2010; Lökman 2011). Moreover, the perception of combat sports and martial arts as violent is debatable (Matthews and Channon 2017). The second benefit from the exploration of martial arts and combat sports, as Sánchez García and Spencer (2014: 2) stated, is the possibility of studying ethnicity and 'race' issues, and the third is that these sports can be seen as a kind of 'secular religion'.

Although the above-listed arguments present martial arts and combat sports as fruitful research fields, they do not explain, in the opinion of the author of this book, the domination of these sports in the research of embodiment. Issues of gender construction or ethnicity can be and have been analysed with reference to other sports disciplines. Therefore, it is difficult to clearly indicate the reasons why martial arts and combat sports have dominated the research; however, several possible causes can be listed. Partly, it could be influenced by Wacquant's publication, which has become 'a cult book' (Sánchez García and Spencer 2014).[1] Moreover, regarding the fact that many of these studies are based on autoethnography, that is, the authors are both the researchers and the learners of a particular sport, one can suppose that the popularity of martial arts and combat sports and the accessibility to them have contributed to the significant number of studies and publications of their results. This accessibility can be understood both as easy access to sports clubs and quite low costs of training (as compared to, for example, tennis and skiing) and as a lack of particular body predispositions necessary to practise these sports, at least at the amateur level (as compared to height in basketball, strength in weight lifting or flexibility in gymnastics).

Apart from martial arts and combat sports, the second sport that has dominated social studies on embodied skills is dance, which is not surprising as, in contrast to the previous research field, the analysis of this discipline has been dominated by female researchers. Their common aspect is the choice of a phenomenological approach as the main theoretical framework. Both Sandra Fraleigh (1987) and Maxime Sheets-Johnstone (1999), whose publications are perceived as ground-breaking in this field (Parviainen 2002: 14), referred to Merleau-Ponty's concept. Fraleigh (1987) described a dancer's knowledge as 'knowing how, bodily lived (experiential) knowledge' (p. 26), whereas Sheets-Johnstone (1999) wrote about non-linguistic and non-propositional physical knowledge, that is, knowing in and through movement.

Phenomenology was chosen as the theoretical framework in many other studies. For example, Tone Pernille Østern (2009) used it in her analysis of a project with the participation of different dancers (with and without disabilities, amateurs and professional). Apart from the field notes from her own teaching, she also used data from video observations and interviews. Leena

Rouhiainen is another author who uses the phenomenological approach, as indicated in the subtitle of her doctoral dissertation, 'Living Transformative Lives: Finnish Freelance Dance Artists Brought into Dialogue with Merleau-Ponty's Phenomenology' (Rouhiainen 2003), and visible in other publications (see, e.g. Rouhiainen *et al.* 2007; Ravn and Rouhiainen 2012). Susanne Ravn (2009), in her investigation of dancers' movement, as well as Jaana Parviainen (2002), in her analysis of bodily (dance) knowledge, used the same theoretical approach. Parviainen (2002) also referred to Polanyi's concept of tacit knowledge to discuss the nature of bodily knowledge and the relations between 'skills' and 'knowledge'.

In publications on dancers' embodiment, one can also find references to Marcel Mauss's and Pierre Bourdieu's theories. For example, Angela Pickard referred to the above authors in her analysis of the process of skills incorporation by practice and training and described a dancer's habitus (Bailey and Pickard 2010; Pickard 2012). Sylvia Faure, in her book *Apprendre par corps. Socio-anthropologie des techniques de danse* [*Learning through the body. Socio-anthropology of dance techniques*] (2000), asked about the relations between body and language and about articulation between modes of incorporation and cognitive (especially reflexive) procedures of learning. In this and other publications (Faure 1999, 2003; Faure and Gosselin 2008), she analysed the embodiment of dance techniques. The author distinguished two ideal types of dance apprenticeship (related to discipline and to singularity) and, as a consequence, two types of memorisation. The first is based on formalised language, technical vocabulary and 'learning by heart', which makes possible the quasi-mechanical reproduction of a particular gesture. The second type of memorisation is less formalised, more unstable and takes into account the context, objects and other people (Faure 1999, 2000).

To answer the question as to why dance has so often been analysed in research on embodied knowledge and learning through the body, one can mention Parviainen's words:

> Knowing in dancing always has something to do with verbal language; nevertheless, it essentially concerns the body's awareness and motility. If we acknowledge that dancers know something and that for the most part their knowing is nonverbal, it leads us to ask, What do they know, and even more importantly, How do they know?
>
> (2002: 13)

The third sport that has been explored in the analysis of embodiment is running. Once again, one can argue that a significant number of publications, mainly autoethnographies, on this sports discipline result from the popularity of running among amateurs. Authors that should be mentioned here are Jacquelyn Allen-Collinson and John Hockey, whose individual and common publications have contributed to the development of the phenomenological approach in social sports studies (Allen-Collinson 2003, 2006, 2008, 2013; Allen-Collinson and Hockey 2001, 2015; Hockey 2006; Hockey and Allen-Collinson 2006, 2007). Phenomenology has also been used as the theoretical approach in studies on other sports, such as football (Hughson and Inglis 2002) and yoga (Morley 2001).

A majority of publications from the social sciences concern embodied knowledge acquisition by amateurs. Rarely have these studies been focused on professional athletes. As an exception, Ole Lund et al.'s publications on elite sports, such as rowing, trampoline jumping or handball, should be noted here (Lund, Ravn and Christensen 2012, 2014; Lund, Musaeus and Christensen 2013). The authors gathered data during interviews and observations and analysed selected case studies from professional athletes' training sessions. It is worth noticing that these studies take into account the learning process in a pair (rowing, trampoline jumping) and in a team (handball), as a significant majority of analyses of acquisition of sports skills as made by sociologists and other representatives of the social sciences concern individual sports. The analyses of embodied knowledge and its acquisition in team sports are scanty and remain a scientific (mainly empirical) challenge. In their case, one should focus not only on the embodied knowledge of an individual player but also on the relation between embodied individuals and their collective tacit knowledge (Collins 2010).

Lund et al. also revealed the important role of other athletes, including the partner in a pair, in the learning process (Lund *et al.* 2012, 2014, 2013). These studies are more focused on mutual learning than on a hierarchical relation between a novice and a master (coach). This kind of analysis constitutes a small part of research on the learning process (Lund *et al.* 2014); however, some examples of these can be found (Galipeau and Trudel 2006; Christensen, Laursen and Sŕrensen 2011; Henriksen, Stambulova and Roessler 2010).

Another author that should be noted here is Ajit Singh, whose doctoral thesis is titled 'Wissenskommunikation im Nachwuchstraining. Eine videographische Studie zur kommunikativen Konstruktion von Körperwissen im Trampolinturnen' [Communicating knowledge in youth training: a videographic study of the communicative construction of embodied knowledge in trampolining] (2016a). Singh's research has been focused on sports training with young athletes, which is very rare in sociology, and drew on the literature output of sociology of the body, sociology of knowledge and sociology of interaction. The videographic analysis of interaction conducted for the purpose of Singh's doctoral dissertation was focused on questions of how embodied knowledge is produced and which forms of its learning, mediating, adopting and practising are made visible and describable (Singh

2016a, see also: Singh 2013, Wedelstaedt and Singh 2017). The focused ethnography (Knoblauch 2005) conducted by Singh seems to be closest to the author's research conducted for this book.

2.3   Research methods

The dominant theoretical paradigm has influenced the choice of methodology used in studies on sports skills embodiment. Most of these studies were based on ethnographic methods, which are perceived as the most fruitful for the study of the process of sports habitus or knowledge incorporation, and of learning body techniques that take place in a specific environment (Spencer 2009; Allen-Collinson 2009). According to Farrer and Whalen-Bridge (2011), 'these methods best serve to help us approach the martial arts experience as opposed to the discursive form that may often displace the most experientially direct ways of knowing' (p. 10).

The studies that were conducted were rarely based on only one research technique, and both types of observation were used in their frameworks: (1) non-participant, during which the learning process (the training sessions) was observed and usually registered, and (2) participant observation (or, as Wacquant proposes, observant participation). The observations, and in the past few years more often video observations, were complemented by qualitative interviews.

A method that has recently become more visible in the social sciences, including sports research, is autoethnography. According to Allen-Collinson (2008: 39), one can even speak about an 'autoethnographic turn' in the analysis of sporting and physical experiences. By using autoethnography, a researcher combines field notes with 'headnotes' (Sanjek 1990); that is, he/she is engaged in the studied activity or process and describes subjective experiences. In Allen-Collinson's publications, one can find numerous examples of detailed autoethnographies, or 'narratives of the self' (Sparkes 2000). This form of inquiry and its critiques (e.g. solipsism, the issue of validity and reliability, 'sample' size) have been discussed by several authors, also with reference to sports studies (Sparkes 2000; Allen-Collinson 2008), therefore they will largely be omitted in this book.

One of the crucial issues in autoethnography is its emphasis on the researcher's body. Although the researcher always uses his/her body during the research process (to prepare a research tool, to conduct an interview, to observe, etc.), in autoethnography, mainly in sports studies, the body is the research tool as well as the research topic. A researcher gathers data through and in the body, but also describes his/her own embodiment experiences. The same can be said about participant observation, where the body becomes a research instrument, or 'a tool of inquiry' (Wacquant 2011), which allows the researcher 'not only to watch and listen but also to feel with the body' (Graham 2014: 66). This attention being drawn to the researcher's corporeality is very important and should also be taken into account in other studies. The emphasis on the role of both the researcher(s)' and participants' embodiments (Rice 2009; Chadwick 2017) can contribute to the development of embodied research methodology (Wellard 2015).

Apprenticeship is another research method that has been distinguished, but it is also a site of inquiry (Downey, Dalidowicz and Manson 2015). Apprenticeship is defined as 'the process of developing from novice to proficiency under the guidance of a skilled expert' (Downey *et al.* 2015: 183). Thus it can be perceived as similar to the process of acquiring habitus. Apprenticeship emphasises the participant dimension, that is, researchers enter into the research field as 'observing participants' rather than as 'participant observers' (Woodward 2008). In this meaning, apprenticeship is also close to autoethnography. Apprenticeship allows one to learn a skill, but also, as Goody (1989: 254–255) and Coy (1989: 2) indicated, to learn about it and learn about how one learns. This gives researchers the possibility to directly study the 'pedagogical work' that is being done on them and with them (Wacquant 2011). Creating the relation between the teacher and the apprentice, besides transferring technical know-how, also offers an embodied understanding of the mechanisms, strategies and emotions connected with specific skill acquisition.

Visual methods have developed in ethnographic studies in the last few years. The main aim is to register the observed activity, although visual methods are also used during the interviews, for example, in the framework of a method called stimulated recall (SR) (You 2009; Houge Mackenzie and Kerr 2012; Nyberg 2015) or during photo elicitation interviews (Curry 1986; Harper 2002). The usability of visual methods in studies with children and young people is presented, among others, in *Pedagogies, Physical Culture, and Visual Methods*, edited by Laura Azzarito and David Kirk (2013).

Although video recording has become more common in ethnographic studies in the field of sport, head-mounted cameras have been used quite rarely. However, a number of research studies based on their use can be noted (see, e.g. Brown *et al.* 2008; Houge Mackenzie and Kerr 2012; Evers 2015). Brown *et al.* (2008) analysed the ethical issues and advantages of the use of head-mounted cameras in an exploration of embodied, multi-sensory ways of knowing through the example of mountain bikers and walkers. In a study conducted by Houge Mackenzie and Kerr (2012) on the experience of river surfing course participants, recordings from head-mounted cameras were presented to the participants during the interviews to receive their commentaries and to reflect on their feelings and thoughts (stimulated recall technique). Clifton Evers (2015) used wearable digital video cameras to explore masculinity in the surfing world. The usefulness of a head-mounted camera as a research tool is also discussed beyond the sports field (see, e.g. Schoonover, Kinsley and Spitler 2016).

Numerous examples of ethnographic studies on sport and embodiment have been collected in two books, *Researching Embodied Sport: Exploring Movement Cultures*, edited by Ian Wellard (2015), and *Ethnographies in Sport and Exercise Research*, edited by Gyozo Molnar and Laura G. Purdy (2016). The former book focuses on both the awareness and the significance of embodiment in the research process, and its aim is to show the utility of the embodied approach for the study of sport and movement cultures. Embodiment is not only considered as a research topic but also refers to the authors' bodies, their role and meaning in sports studies and the authors' incorporated challenges during the gathering of data. In the latter book, beyond the empirical studies one can also find considerations on a theoretical framework, the history of ethnography in sport and exercise research, and a prognosis for its development. Both books present the methodological challenges that the authors had to face and provide a significant amount of practical advice to overcome those challenges.

The studies and publications presented here emphasise the role of researchers' embodiment in the research process. This embodied approach, which is visible in ethnography, including autoethnography, has many advantages. It breaks the dichotomy between the mind and the body, it takes into account the embodied consciousness of both the researcher and the individual being researched, and it is sensitive to all of the senses of the embodied experience. Some authors even claim that 'embodied practice' is necessary to conduct an analysis of the physical activities, and they suggest to conduct 'an ethnography from the body' (Samudra 2008: 666).

While the advantages of this kind of research can be appreciated, one also has to remember its limitations. The same skill is understood, learnt and acquired differently by different persons. Therefore, studies limited to one researcher and one sport or even one skill will always provide quite limited knowledge. In the study conducted by the book's author and her research team, differences were observed even among children who were one to two years older/younger than others, as well as between different levels of sports training sessions.

Moreover, the majority (if not all) of the studies described above concern only one discipline. This means that the authors conducted research in only one discipline, such as capoeira, dance or running. Only a few authors analysed more disciplines, but not in the framework of the same research project (Nyberg 2014a; Lund *et al.* 2012, 2013, 2014). In the current study, conducted in both Poland and France, data from three types of sport were gathered and analysed with the same research tools. This allowed comparison of the data from the perspective of tacit knowledge. Because five investigators participated, it was also possible to gather different voices, both male and female, concerning the embodied process of apprenticeship with reference to three different sports disciplines.

The domination of the phenomenological approach, and the autoethnography, apprenticeship and observant participation methods related to it, results in skills transmission being analysed mainly from the apprentice's experience and his/her point of view. Another consequence of these theoretical and methodological choices is the omission of children and youth in studies on embodied knowledge. There is a significant number of publications which concern physical education and as such are focused on children but do not use, with a few exceptions (Nyberg and Larsson 2014; Ma 2015), the concept of tacit knowledge.

In the research that will be presented in the following chapters, knowledge transfer is analysed from a master's (coach's) perspective, that is, from the perspective of a person who transfers and communicates knowledge. Therefore, contrary to most of the research conducted so far, it is the teaching process rather than the learning process that is the central focus. Moreover, the current study concerns the sport of children and youth, as observation of the training sessions with these age groups allows analysis of the transfer of tacit knowledge to a much larger extent. Although many of the authors mentioned above have emphasised the difficulties of verbalising embodied knowledge, they have not analysed these difficulties in a detailed manner. These difficulties, in turn, are the focus of this book, which analyses the limits of tacit knowledge verbalisation and the relations between different types of communication that are used during sports training sessions.

The research project conducted here tried to overcome some of the limitations that were observed in previous studies, such as the focus on one sports discipline or the lack of voices of other novices. It undoubtedly also has its own limitations and, as such, can be treated as a lesson for further studies.

Note

1 Wacquant's book is one of the most often discussed books on the subject in the literature. Special issues of journals, such as *Qualitative Sociology* [2005] and *Theory and Psychology* [2009], as well as numerous academic symposiums, have been organised around this book and the epistemological and methodological implications of Wacquant's research.

References

Allen-Collinson, J., 2003, 'Running into injury time: Distance running and temporality', *Sociology of Sport Journal*, 20(4), 331–350.
Allen-Collinson, J., 2006, 'Running together: Some ethnomethodological considerations', *Ethnographic Studies*, 8, 17–29.

Allen-Collinson, J., 2008, 'Running the routes together corunning and knowledge in action', *Journal of Contemporary Ethnography*, 37(1), 38–61.

Allen-Collinson, J., 2009, 'Sporting embodiment: Sports studies and the (continuing) promise of phenomenology', *Qualitative Research in Sport and Exercise*, 1(3), 279–296.

Allen-Collinson, J., 2013, 'Narratives of and from a running-woman's body: Feminist phenomenological perspectives on running embodiment', *Leisure Studies Association Newsletter*, 95, 41–48.

Allen-Collinson, J. and Hockey, J., 2001 'Runners' tales: Autoethnography, injury and narrative', *Auto/Biography*, 9(1–2), 95–106.

Allen-Collinson, J. and Hockey, J., 2011, 'Feeling the way: Notes towards a haptic phenomenology of distance running and scuba diving', *International Review for the Sociology of Sport*, 46, 330–345.

Allen-Collinson, J. and Hockey, J., 2015, 'From a certain point of view: Sensory phenomenological envisionings of running space and place', *Journal of Contemporary Ethnography*, 44(1), 63–83.

Andersson, J., Östman, L. and Öhman, M., 2013, 'I am sailing – towards a transactional analysis of "body techniques"', *Sport, Education and Society*, 3(18), 1–19.

Ávila da Costa, L., McNamee, M. and Lacerda, T.O., 2014, 'Physical education as an aestheticethical educational project', *European Physical Education Review*, 29, 1–14.

Azzarito, L. and Kirk, D. (eds.), 2013, *Pedagogies, Physical Culture, and Visual Methods*, Routledge, Abingdon, UK.

Bailey, R. and Pickard, A., 2010, 'Body learning: Examining the processes of skill learning in dance', *Sport, Education and Society*, 15(3), 367–382.

Bourdieu, P., 1977, *Outline of a Theory of Practice*, Cambridge University Press, Cambridge.

Breivik, G., 2008, 'Bodily movement – the fundamental dimensions', *Sport, Ethics and Philosophy*, 2, 337–352.

Breivik, G., 2014, 'Sporting knowledge and the problem of knowing how', *Journal of the Philosophy of Sport*, 41(2), 143–162.

Brown, K., Dilley, R. and Marshall, K., 2008, 'Using a head-mounted video camera to understand social worlds and experiences', *Sociological Research Online*, 13(6), DOI: 10.5153/sro.1818.

Brown, T.D. and Payne, P.G., 2009, 'Conceptualizing the phenomenology of movement in physical education: Implications for pedagogical inquiry and development', *Quest*, 61, 418–441.

Casey, E., 1998, 'The ghost of embodiment: On bodily habitudes', in D. Welton (ed.), *Body and Flesh: A Philosophical Reader*, pp. 207–226, Blackwell Publishers Inc., Oxford.

Chadwick, R., 2017, 'Embodied methodologies: Challenges, reflections and strategies', *Qualitative Research*, 17(1), 54–74.

Christensen, M.K., Laursen, D.N. and Sřrensen, J.K., 2011, 'Situated learning in youth elite football: A Danish case study of talented male under-18 football players', *Physical Education and Sport Pedagogy*, 16(2), 1–16.

Collins, H.M., 2010, *Tacit and Explicit Knowledge*, University of Chicago Press, Chicago.

Coy, M. (ed.), 1989, *Apprenticeship: From Theory to Method and Back Again*, State University of New York Press, Albany, NY.

Crossley, N., 2001, 'The phenomenological habitus and its construction', *Theory and Society*, 30, 81–120.

Crossley, N., 2004a, 'Ritual: Body technique and (inter)subjectivity', in K. Schilbrack (ed.), *Thinking Through Ritual: Philosophical Perspective*, pp. 31–51, Routledge, London.

Crossley, N., 2004b, 'The circuit trainer's habitus', *Body and Society*, 10(1), 37–69.

Crossley, N., 2005, 'Mapping reflexive body techniques: On body modification and maintenance', *Body and Society*, 11(1), 1–35.

Curry, T.J., 1986, 'A visual method of studying sports: The photo-elicitation interview', *Sociology of Sport Journal*, 3(3), 204–216.

de Grave, J.-M., 2001, *Initiation rituelle et arts martiaux: trois écoles de kanuragan Javanais [The Ritual Initiation and Martial Arts: Three Schools of Javanese Kanuragan]*, Association Archipel, Paris.

de Grave, J.-M., 2011, 'The training of perception in Javanese martial arts', in D.S. Farrer and J. Whalen-Bridge (eds.), *Martial Arts as Embodied Knowledge: Asian Traditions in a Transnational World*, pp. 123–144, Suny Press, Albany.

Delamont, S. and Stephens, N., 2008, 'Up on the roof: The embodied habitus of diasporic capoeira', *Cultural Sociology*, 2, 57–74.

Dilley, R., 1989, 'Secrets and skills: Apprenticeship among Tukolor weavers', in M.W. Coy (ed.), *Apprenticeship: From Theory to Method and Back Again*, pp. 181–198, Suny Press, Albany, NY.

Downey, G., 2005a, *Learning Capoeira: Lessons in Cunning from an Afro-Brazilian Art*, Oxford University Press, Oxford.

Downey, G., 2005b, 'Educating the eyes: Biocultural anthropology and physical education', *Anthropology in Action*, 12(2), 56–71.

Downey, G., 2007, 'Seeing with a "sideways glance": Visuomotor "knowing" and the plasticity of perception', in M. Harris (ed.), *Ways of Knowing: Anthropological Approaches to Crafting Experience and Knowledge*, pp. 222–224, Berghahn, New York.

Downey, G., 2008, 'Scaffolding imitation in capoeira: Physical education and enculturation in an Afro-Brazilian art', *American Anthropologist*, 110, 204–213.

Downey, G., 2010, '"Practice without theory": A neuroanthropological perspective on embodied learning', *Journal of the Royal Anthropological Institute*, 16, 22–40.

Downey, G., Dalidowicz, M. and Manson, P.H., 2015, 'Apprenticeship as method: Embodied learning in ethnographic practice', *Qualitative Research*, 15(2), 183–200.

Evans, J., Davies, B. and Rich, E., 2014, 'We/you can tell talk from matter: A conversation with Håkan Larsson and Mikael Quennerstedt', *Sport, Education and Society*, 19(5), 652–665.

Evers, C., 2015, 'Researching action sport with a GoPro™ camera: An embodied and emotional mobile video tale of the sea, masculinity, and men-who-surf', in I. Wellard (ed.), *Researching Embodied Sport: Exploring Movement Cultures*, pp. 145–162, Routledge, London.

Farrer, D.S., 2007, 'The perils and pitfalls of performance ethnography', *International Sociological Association: E-Bulletin*, 17–26. Viewed 7 November 2016 from www.sagepub.net/isa/resources/files/e-bulletin6final_edit.pdf#page=17

Farrer, D.S. and Whalen-Bridge, J. (eds.), 2011, *Martial Arts as Embodied Knowledge: Asian Traditions in a Transnational World*, Suny Press, Albany.

Faure, S., 1999, 'Les processus d'incorporation et d'appropriation des savoir-faire du danseur' [The process of incorporation and appropriation of the dancer's know-how], *Éducation et Sociétés: Revue internationale de sociologie de l'éducation*, 4(2), 75–90.

Faure, S., 2000, *Apprendre par corps. Socio-anthropologie des techniques de danse* [*Learning through the Body: Socio-Anthropology of the Dance Techniques*], La Dispute, Paris.

Faure, S., 2003, 'Apprentissages et motricités de la danse chorégraphiée' [Learing and motor skills of choreographed dance], in M. Kail and M. Fayol (eds.), *Les sciences cognitives et l'école* [*The Cognitive Sciences and School*], pp. 415–442, Presses Universitaires de France, Paris.

Faure, S. and Gosselin, A.S., 2008, 'Apprendre par corps: le concept à l'épreuve de l'enquête empirique. Exemple des jeunes danseurs des favelas' [Learning through the body: The concept tested by an empirical survey: Example of young dancers of the favelas], *Regards sociologiques*, 35, 27–36.

Fisette, J.L., 2011, 'Exploring how girls navigate their embodied identities in physical education', *Physical Education and Sport Pedagogy*, 16(2), 179–196.

Fraleigh, S., 1987, *Dance and the Lived Body*, University of Pittsburgh Press, Pittsburgh.

Galipeau, J. and Trudel, P., 2006, 'Athlete learning in a community of practice: Is there a role for the coach?', in R.L. Jones (ed.), *The Sports Coach as Educator: Re-Conceptualising Sports Coaching*, pp. 77–94, Routledge, Abingdon.

Goody, E.N., 1989, 'Learning, apprenticeship and the division of labor', in M.W. Coy (ed.), *Apprenticeship: From Theory to Method and Back Again*, pp. 233–256, State University of New York Press, Albany, NY.

Graham, E., 2014, '"There is not try in tae kwon do": Reflexive body techniques in action', in R. Sanchez García and D.C. Spencer (eds.), *Fighting Scholars: Habitus and Ethnographies of Martial Arts and Combat Sports*, pp. 63–78, Anthem Press, London and New York.

Guérandel, C. and Mennesson, Ch., 2007, 'Gender construction in judo interaction', *International Review for the Sociology of Sport*, 42(2), 167–186.

Harper, D., 2002, 'Talking about pictures: A case for photo elicitation', *Visual Studies*, 17(1), 13–26.

Henriksen, K., Stambulova, N. and Roessler, K.K., 2010, 'Holistic approach to athletic talent development environments: A successful sailing milieu', *Psychology of Sport and Exercise*, 11(3), 212–222.

Herzfeld, M., 2004, *The Body Impolitic: Artisans and Artifice in the Global Hierarchy of Value*, University of Chicago Press, Chicago.

Hockey, J., 2006, 'Sensing the run: The senses and distance running', *Senses and Society*, 1(2), 183–202.

Hockey, J. and Allen-Collinson, J., 2006, 'Seeing the way: Visual sociology and the distance runner's perspective', *Visual Studies: Journal of the International Visual Sociology Association*, 21(1), 70–81.

Hockey, J. and Allen-Collinson, J., 2007, 'Grasping the phenomenology of sporting bodies', *International Review for the Sociology of Sport*, 42(2), 115–131.

Hogeveen, B., 2011, 'Skilled coping and sport: Promises of phenomenology', *Sport, Ethics and Philosophy*, 5(3), 245–255.

Houge Mackenzie, S. and Kerr, J.K., 2012, 'Head-mounted cameras and stimulated recall in qualitative sport research', *Qualitative Research In Sport, Exercise And Health*, 4(1), 51–61.

Hughson, J. and Inglis, D., 2002, 'Inside the beautiful game: Towards a Merleau-Pontian phenomenology of soccer play', *Journal of the Philosophy of Sport*, 29, 1–15.

Ivinson, G.M., 2012, 'Skills in motion: Boys' trail motorbiking activities as transitions into working class masculinity in a post-industrial locale', *Sport, Education and Society*, 19(5), 605–620.

Janik, A., 1988, 'Tacit knowledge, working life and scientific method', in B. Göranzon and I. Josefson (eds.), *Knowledge, Skill and Artificial Intelligence*, pp. 53–63, Springer-Verlag, London.

Jespersen, E., 2003, 'Bodyscapes of the act of learning', *Theoria et Historia Scientiarium*, 3, 209–221.

Kerry, D.S. and Armour, K.M., 2000, 'Sport sciences and the promise of phenomenology: Philosophy, method, and insight', *Quest*, 52, 1–17.

Knoblauch, H., 2005, 'Focused ethnography', *Forum Qualitative Sozialforschung/ Forum: Qualitative Social Research*, 6(3). Viewed 7 November 2016 from www. qualitative-research.net/index.php/fqs/article/view/20/43

Kresse, K. and Marchand, T.H.J., 2009, 'Introduction: Knowing in practice', *Africa*, 79(1), 1–16.

Larsson, H. and Quennerstedt, M., 2012, 'Understanding movement: A sociocultural approach to exploring moving humans', *Quest*, 64(4), 283–298.

Law, M., 2008, *The Pyjama Game: A Journey into Judo*, Aurum Press, London.

Lökman, P., 2011, 'Becoming aware of gendered embodiment: Female beginners learning Aikido', in E. Kennedy and P. Markula (eds.), *Women and Exercise: The Body, Health and Consumerism*, pp. 266–279, Routledge, New York.

Lund, O., Musaeus, P. and Christensen, M.K., 2013, 'Shared deliberate practice: A case study of elite handball team training', *Athletic Insight*, 5(2), 211–228.

Lund, O., Ravn, S. and Christensen, M.K., 2012, 'Learning by joining the rhythm apprenticeship learning in elite double sculls rowing', *Scandinavian Sport Studies Forum*, 3, 167–188.

Lund, O., Ravn, S. and Christensen, M.K., 2014, 'Jumping together: Apprenticeship learning among elite trampoline athletes', *Physical Education and Sport Pedagogy*, 19(4), 383–397.

Ma, L., 2015, 'Analysis on Existence and Transmission of Tacit Knowledge in Sports Teaching', The International Conference on Education Technology and Economic Management, 14–15 March 2015, Beijing. Viewed 23 September 2016 from www. atlantis-press.com/php/pub.php?publication=icetem-15andframe=http%3A// www.atlantis-press.com/php/welcome.php%3Fpublication%3Dicetem-15

Marchand, T.H.J., 2001, *Minaret Building and Apprenticeship in Yemen*, Curzon, London.

Martínková, I. and Parry, J. (eds.), 2012, *Phenomenological Approach to Sport Studies*, Routledge, Abingdon, UK.

Matthews, Ch.R., 2015, 'Being nosey: The body as an effective but flawed tool for research', in I. Wellard (ed.), *Researching Embodied Sport: Exploring Movement Cultures*, pp. 130–144, Routledge, Abingdon, UK.

Matthews, Ch.R. and Channon, A., 2017, 'Understanding sports violence: Revisiting foundational explorations', *Sport in Society*, 7, 751–767.

Matthews, D., 2002, *Looking For a Fight: How a Writer Took On the Boxing World from the Inside*, Headline, London.

Mauss, M., 1973[1935], 'Techniques of the body', *Economy and Society*, 2(1), 70–88.

Mennesson, Ch., 2000, '"Hard" women and "soft" women: The social construction of identities among female boxers', *International Review for the Sociology of Sport*, 35(1), 21–33.

Mennesson, Ch., 2004, 'Être une femme dans un sport masculine' [To be a woman in masculine sport], *Sociétés Contemporaines*, 55, 69–90.

Merchant, S., 2011, 'The body and the senses: Visual methods, videography and the submarine sensorium', *Body and Society*, 17, 53–72.

Merleau-Ponty, M., 2002[1948], *Phenomenology of Perception*, Routledge, London.

Molnar, G. and Purdy, L.G. (eds.), 2016, *Ethnographies in Sport and Exercise Research*, Routledge, Abingdon, UK.

Morley, J., 2001, 'Inspiration and expiration: Yoga practice through Merleau-Ponty's phenomenology of the body', *Philosophy East and West*, 51(1), 73–82.

Nyberg, G., 2014a, *Ways of Knowing in Ways of Moving: A Study of the Meaning of Capability to Move*, Stockholm University, Stockholm.

Nyberg, G., 2015, 'Developing a "somatic velocimeter" – the practical knowledge of freeskiers', *Qualitative Research in Sport, Exercise and Health*, 7(1), 109–124.

Nyberg, G. and Larsson, H., 2014, 'Exploring "what" to learn in physical education', *Physical Education and Sport Pedagogy*, 19(2), 123–135.

O'Connor, E., 2005, 'Embodied knowledge: The experience of meaning and the struggle towards proficiency in glassblowing', *Ethnography*, 6(2), 183–204.

Østern, T.P., 2009, *Meaning-Making in the Dance Laboratory: Exploring Dance Improvisation with Differently Bodied Dancers*, Theater Academy, Helsinki.

Oualhaci, A., 2014, 'Les savoirs dans la salle de boxe thaï. Transmission de savoirs, hiérarchies et reconnaissance locale dans une salle de boxe thaï en banlieue populaire' [Knowledge in Thai boxing gym: Transmission of knowledge, hierarchies and local recognition in a Thai boxing gym located in a low income suburb], *Revue d'anthropologie des connaissances*, 8(4), 807–832.

Parviainen, J., 2002, 'Bodily knowledge: Epistemological reflections on dance', *Dance Research Journal*, 34(1), 11–26.

Parviainen, J. and Aromaa, J., 2015, 'Bodily knowledge beyond motor skills and physical fitness: A phenomenological description of knowledge formation in physical training', *Sport, Education and Society*, DOI: 10.1080/13573322.2015.1054273.

Pickard, A., 2012, 'Schooling the dancer: The evolution of an identity as a ballet dancer', *Research In Dance Education*, 13(1), 25–46.

Pink, S., 2009, *Doing Sensory Ethnography*, SAGE Publications Ltd., London.

Polanyi, M., 1966, *The Tacit Dimension*, University of Chicago Press, Chicago.

Ravn, S., 2009, *Sensing Movement, Living Spaces: An Investigation of Movement Based on the Lived Experience of 13 Professional Dancers*, VDM Verlag, Saarbrucken.

Embodied sports knowledge transmission 41

Ravn, S. and Rouhiainen, L. (eds.), 2012, *Dance Spaces: Practices of Movement*. University Press of Southern Denmark, Odense.

Rice, C., 2009, 'Imagining the other? Ethical challenges of researching and writing women's embodied lives', *Feminism and Psychology*, 19(2), 245–266.

Rouhiainen, L., 2003, *Living Transformative Lives: Finnish Freelance Dance Artists Brought into Dialogue with Merleau-Ponty's Phenomenology*, Theatre Academy, Helsinki.

Rouhiainen, L., Anttila, E., Heimonen, K., Hämäläinen, S., Kauppila, K. and Salosaari, P. (eds.), 2007, 'Ways of knowing in dance and art', in *Acta Scenica*, p. 19, Theatre Academy, Helsinki.

Ryle, G., 1949, *The Concept of Mind*, London: Routledge.

Samudra, J., 2008, 'Memory in our body: Thick participation and the translation of kinesthetic experience', *American Ethnologist*, 35, 665–681.

Sánchez García, R. and Spencer, D.C. (eds.), 2014, *Fighting Scholars: Habitus and Ethnographies of Martial Arts and Combat Sports*, Anthem Press, London and New York.

Sanjek, R. (ed.), 1990, *Fieldnotes: The Making of Anthropology*, Cornell University Press, Ithaca, NY.

Schindler, L., 2009, 'The production of <<vis-ability>>: An ethnographic video analysis of a martial arts class', in U. Kissmann (ed.), *Video Interaction Analysis: Methods and Methodology*, pp. 135–154, Peter Lang, Frankfurt am Main.

Schneider, S., 2010, 'Learning India's martial arts of Kalarippayattu', *Journal of Asian Martial Arts*, 19(3), 46–63.

Schoonover, D., Kinsley, K.M. and Spitler, J., 2016, 'GoPro as an ethnographic tool: A wayfinding study in an academic library', *Journal of Access Services*, 13(1), 7–23.

Sheets-Johnstone, M., 1999, *The Primacy of Movement*, John Benjamins Publishing Company, Amsterdam, Philadelphia.

Sheets-Johnstone, M., 2000, 'Kinetic tactile-kinesthetic bodies: Ontogenetical foundations of apprenticeship learning', *Human Studies*, 23, 343–370.

Simpson, E., 2006, 'Apprenticeship in Western India', *Journal of the Royal Anthropological Institute*, 12, 151–171.

Singh, A., 2013, 'Die Qualität der Spannung. Eine videographische Untersuchung zur visuellen Kom-munikation von verkörpertem Wissen im Trampolinturnen' [The quality of tension: A videographic study in visual communication of embodied knowledge in trampoline jumping], *Soziale Welt*, 64, 97–114.

Singh, A., 2016a, Wissenskommunikation im Nachwuchstraining. Eine videographische Studie zur kommunikativen Konstruktion von Körperwissen im Trampolinturnen [Communicating knowledge in professional training with young athletes: A videography study of the communicative construction of embodied knowledge], Ph.D thesis. Universität Bayreuth.

Sparkes, A., 2000, 'Autoethnography and narratives of the self: Reflections on criteria in action', *Sociology of Sport Journal*, 17, 21–43.

Sparkes, A., 2009, 'Ethnography and the senses: Challenges and possibilities', *Qualitative Research in Sport, Exercise and Health*, 1, 21–35.

Sparkes, A., 2010, 'Performing the ageing body and the importance of place: Some brief autoethnographic moments', in B. Humberstone (ed.), *'When I Am Oldy'*

Third Age and Leisure Research: Principles and Practice, pp. 21–32, LSA publication, Leisure Studies Association, Eastbourne.

Sparkes, A., 2016, 'Ethnography as a sensual way of being: Methodological and representational challenges', in G. Molnar and L.G. Purdy (eds.), *Ethnographies in Sport and Exercise Research*, pp. 45–58, Routledge, Abingdon, UK.

Spencer, D.C., 2009, 'Habit(us), body techniques and body callusing: An ethnography of mixed martial arts', *Body and Society*, 15(4), 119–143.

Spencer, D.C., 2011, *Ultimate Fighting and Embodiment: Violence, Gender and Mixed Martial Arts*, Routledge, New York.

Spencer, D.C., 2012, 'Narratives of despair and loss: Pain, injury and masculinity in the sport of mixed arts', *Qualitative Research in Sport, Health and Exercise*, 4(1), 117–137.

Standal, Ø.F. and Engelsrud, G., 2013, 'Researching embodiment in movement contexts: A phenomenological approach', *Sport, Education and Society*, 18(2), 154–166.

Stephens, N. and Delamont, S., 2006, 'Balancing the berimbau: Embodied ethnographic understanding', *Qualitative Inquiry*, 12(2), 316–339.

Stephens, N. and Delamont, S., 2009, '"They start to get malicia": Teaching tacit and technical knowledge', *British Journal of Sociology of Education*, 30(5), 537–548.

Wacquant, L., 1989, 'Corps et âme: notes ethnographiques d'un apprenti-boxeur' [Body and soul: Ethnographic notes of apprentice boxer], *Actes de la recherche en science sociales*, 80, 33–67.

Wacquant, L., 1995, 'Pugs at work: Bodily capital and bodily labour among professional boxers', *Body and Society*, 1(1), 65–94.

Wacquant, L., 2004, *Body and Soul: Notebooks of an Apprentice Boxer*, Oxford University Press, New York.

Wacquant, L., 2005, 'Carnal connections: On embodiment, apprenticeship, and membership', *Qualitative Sociology*, 28, 445–474.

Wacquant, L., 2011, 'Habitus as topic and tool: Reflections on becoming a prizefighter', *Qualitative Research in Psychology*, 8, 81–92.

Wedelstaedt, U.V. and Singh, A., 2017, 'Intercorporeal with the imaginary – training body schemes in trampolining and boxing', in C. Meyer and U.V. Wedelstaedt (eds.), *Moving Bodies in Interaction – Interacting Bodies in Motion: Intercorporeal and Interkinesthetic Enaction in Sports*, John Benjamins, Amsterdam.

Wellard, I. (ed.), 2015, *Researching Embodied Sport: Exploring Movement Cultures*, Routledge, Abingdon and New York.

Woodward, K., 2008, 'Hanging out and hanging about: Insider/outsider research in the sport of boxing', *Ethnography*, 9(4), 536–560.

You, J.A., 2009, 'Teaching beginning dance classes in higher education: Learning to teach from an expert dance educator', *International Journal of Education and the Arts*, 10(23). Viewed 23 September 2016 from www.ijea.org/v10n23

3 Methodology for studying tacit knowledge in the field of sports

3.1 The project described

If sports skills and techniques can be communicated, verbally or non-verbally, by a trainer to a novice, they can also be communicated to a researcher (Standal and Engelsrud 2013). The process of their transfer was explored within this research project whose main aim was to analyse tacit knowledge transmission with reference to sports skills.

As shown by Polanyi's (1966) example of car driving, the more experience a learner gains, the less a teacher's presence is required. While at the beginning of the teaching process interactions between a learner and an instructor are very intense, their number decreases with time. As a consequence, the process of knowledge transmission is more difficult to observe and study. Therefore, to increase the chances of being able to see and analyse this process, this research project was focused on the sports trainings of children and youth (6–14 years old). This age group was chosen in order to observe novices who are at the beginning of their sports education, as well as athletes who already have some, although still quite limited, experience. It was also assumed that gender differences should be more visible in the case of teenagers as a result of puberty and physiological aspects as well as gender stereotypes and how girls and boys are perceived in the field of sport (Young 1990; McDonagh and Pappano 2008). The prevalence of these gender differences causes coaches to differentiate their attitude and training methods (e.g. the ways of giving commands) towards girls and boys (Jakubowska 2014).

As for the enormous diversification of sport disciplines, the research was limited to three disciplines: (1) athletics (more precisely, running, throwing and jumping, because these are practised by children and youth), (2) swimming and (3) judo. The criteria for the selection of disciplines were: (1) type of skills required in these sports disciplines, (2) different use of the body, (3) relation to the rival's body (contact vs. non-contact sports), (4) space (indoor vs. outdoor sports), and (5) place of competition (track, swimming pool and mat). It was also important that these disciplines are popular among children and young people, are taught in sports schools or classes and are practised at a significant number of sports clubs (beyond athletics).

The research project consisted of two stages. It started with content analysis of training manuals, which had two main purposes:

1   to look at the explicit knowledge, that is, written instructions on how to teach swimming, judo and athletics, and
2   to reveal the relations and boundaries between verbal and non-verbal (visual) information.

Fifteen training manuals were chosen (five from each discipline). The manuals were selected by sports coaches who were asked for a list of manuals that they used and/or recommended. Additionally, the choice of manuals was made on the basis of the literature included in the syllabi of coaching courses at academies of physical education in Poland. The limits of this book do not allow presenting this stage in detail.

The main stage of the study on which this book is focused was inspired by Werner Sperschneider's (2007) product design research. In this stage, three methods were used to gather the data: (1) situated interviews with experts, (2) apprenticeship and (3) video-based observations with the use of GoPro cameras. These methods can be seen as three requests that the researchers asked the coaches. During the situated interviews, they were asked, *Tell me what you do*; during the apprenticeship, they were asked *Teach me how*; and during the video observations, they were told *Show me your everyday procedure* (Sperschneider 2007). From a formal point of view, not all persons who work with children can be called coaches. Some of them, both in Poland and in France, are PE teachers or instructors. However, the word 'coach' will be used considering the lack of differences in their behaviour and for clarity of the analysis.

The research team consisted of six persons: the principal investigator (the book's author) and five investigators – four PhD students (two women and two men) and one female MA student. All of the research tools were created by the book's author, who was also responsible for the analysis of the gathered data. She also did the French part of the fieldwork. The investigators conducted the situated interviews and observations in Poland, took part in the apprenticeship and coded a part of the gathered data to guarantee research reliability.

3.2   Situated interviews with experts

Situated interviews are qualitative, semi-structured interviews conducted in the usual environment. Because they are 'situated', the informants have direct access to the place of practice and to its details (Ylirisku and Buur

2007; Pink 2009). For this research project, the situated interviews with coaches working with children and young people were conducted in sports venues, such as gymnasiums and swimming pools. The coaches were considered as experts in the process of tacit knowledge transmission. It was assumed that, due to their experience both as coaches and as former athletes (in the majority of cases), they would be able to, at least to some extent, articulate and explain the tacit knowledge and to discern the details and nuances of that knowledge (Janik 1996; Carlgren 2007; Magill 2011).

The interview guide consisted of five parts that were focused on (1) the coaches' occupational and athletic experience, (2) the teaching methods, (3) (non)verbal communication, (4) the training manuals and (5) gender issues (Appendix A). Although all parts provided interesting data, the book refers mainly to data gathered during the second and third parts of the interviews. Apart from the interview guide, the investigators also obtained auxiliary materials: (1) a list of teaching methods described in the training manuals which could be helpful in the second part of the interview and (2) drawings from the training manuals, which were used in the fourth part of the interview.

A total of fifteen interviews (five from each of the studied sports disciplines) were conducted by the five investigators. The coaches included both women (7) and men (8), and they had various professional experience, from three to thirty-three years (13 years on average). They had been working in sports clubs and as PE teachers. Most of the interview participants had worked only with children; however, several also had professional experience with senior athletes. The coaches, with a few exceptions, had been athletes in the past. Each interview was audio recorded and then transcribed verbatim by the person who had conducted it.

3.3 Apprenticeship

Apprenticeship, as mentioned above, is a process of developing skills under the guidance of a skilled expert. It can also be used as a method to gather more hidden knowledge, including non-verbal, practical and emotional aspects (Downey, Dalidowicz and Manson 2015). In the framework of the research that was conducted, one cannot speak about a real apprenticeship but rather about its sample. The investigators did not participate in the long process of skills learning or improvement. Their training sessions were conducted only once, directly after the interviews. The research team's members asked the coaches to teach them a selected sports technique. In the case of athletics, this was the sprint start; in judo, a selected throw; and in swimming, the hand movement in the crawl stroke (without being in the water). It should be stressed that some of the coaches were sceptical about the idea of conducting a short, one-time training session, although all of them undertook this task. In this phase, the investigators' gender could have been important (assumed gender differences in the process of knowledge transmission); therefore, homogeneous and gender-mixed pairs of respondents and researchers were created before this stage of the project was started. The principal investigator asked the investigators to make notes as soon as possible after the short training session to describe the process of knowledge transmission and to share their reflections. Additionally, after this part of the research, the research team met to gather the investigators' experiences and their remarks from the fieldwork.

The use of apprenticeship had two aims. First, to participate in the process of knowledge transmission in order to recognise and experience the ways of transferring sports techniques that are used by coaches. It was assumed that due to this the researchers would become more attentive, see more during the video-based observations and provide more detailed information in their field notes. In this meaning, apprenticeship has been perceived as education of attention (Gieser 2008), during which 'novices are instructed to feel this, taste that, or watch out for the other thing' (Ingold 2000: 22). The second aim of this research task was to verify, thanks to the field notes, to what extent it is possible to transfer one's own embodied experiences into a verbalised and communicated form.

3.4   Video-based observation with the use of GoPro cameras

The third method used during the fieldwork was video-based observation. This phase of the research was also conducted in France, as initially data were to be gathered only in Poland. However, due to a fellowship that was received from the Foundation Maison de Sciences de l'Homme (international mobility DEA Programme), the book's author could also conduct research in France. This country was chosen for three main reasons. First, because of its social heterogeneity, which is also visible in the field of sports. Polish society is very homogeneous, and it is not yet possible to conduct the study from an intersectionality perspective on the cumulative impact of race, ethnicity and gender in that country. The influence of these will be discussed in other, future publications. Second, the choice of France was dictated by the tradition of research on embodiment and embodied practices in the French social sciences (e.g. Mauss 1973[1935]; Merleau-Ponty 2002[1948]; Bourdieu 1977), which is being continued today (see, e.g. Faure 2000; Andrieu, Paintendre and Burel 2014). And, third, the author of this book speaks French, which allowed her to conduct the research in France and to analyse the video recordings. The other methods were not used in France because only the principal investigator went to France and stayed there only six weeks. In France, training sessions for children and youth are usually organised twice a week (most often on Tuesdays or Wednesdays and Fridays) at the same hour;

therefore, there was not enough time to use the other methods. The second reason was also the language barrier. Although, as was mentioned, the author speaks French fluently, the sports coaches' utterances were based on specific sports jargon and were at least partly incomprehensible. As a consequence, interviews would have been difficult to conduct.

All observations, both in Poland and France, took place during training sessions in sports venues, such as clubs, gymnasiums in schools and swimming pools. In the case of athletics, the observations were conducted both inside and outside sports halls, and in judo and swimming, only inside them. The observations lasted from thirty minutes for the youngest age group to ninety minutes for the oldest group. Most of the training sessions, and thus observations, lasted one hour. The training sessions were recorded on head-mounted (GoPro) cameras worn by the coaches. Additionally, field notes based on the guidelines were taken by the researchers. The investigators were asked to provide basic information regarding each training session (sport discipline, number and gender of the learners, coach's gender, place) and to describe the course of the training session by paying particular attention to some aspects, such whether the coach only explained or also demonstrated a technique, or whether when teaching a particular technique the coach split it into the small elements (Appendix B).

All coaches who took part in the situated interviews were asked to participate in this part of the research; however, only seven of them agreed to do so. In France, none of the coaches who were asked to participate in this stage of the research refused. It is difficult to clearly explain the difference between these two types of attitudes; it could have resulted from individual features (of the researchers and of the coaches), more openness to a foreign researcher, a different culture, and so forth. In Poland, although not all of the reasons for the refusals were recognised, some of them resulted from the request to record a training session being perceived as a kind of control or audit during which the coach's work would be evaluated. Therefore, seven coaches continued their participation in the research project and the rest were selected only for the video-recording phase of the research.

In the case of both the situated interviews and the observations, the coaches were chosen on the basis of their availability and then by using the snowball method. In France, the research process was supported by the University of Toulouse because of the researchers' network and thanks to a recommendation letter signed by the CRESCO laboratory's director, Christine Mennesson. The book's author was introduced to the main coach of an athletics club, who helped her to conduct observations in this discipline. In the case of both judo and swimming, the author visited sports clubs located in Toulouse and asked their authorities, and then individual coaches, for permission to conduct the observations.

Thirty-nine (13 for each discipline) video-based observations were conducted in both Poland and France. The Polish observations were conducted in the city of Poznań ($n = 18$) and in the Greater Poland Voivodeship ($n = 6$), whereas the French observations were conducted in the city of Toulouse ($n = 15$). The observations complied with all standards related to research involving children as well as with general ethical guidelines for research.

As was mentioned above, each training session was recorded with the use of a head-mounted GoPro camera. Usually the recording started at the beginning of the training session and finished at its end; however, some coaches stated that there was no sense in recording the warm-up and/or the cool-down, therefore these parts of the training sessions were not included in the video recordings. It should also be noted that several coaches turned off the cameras for a while or asked to finish the recording in particular situations during the training sessions. The first of these were breaks, which were probably perceived as not important from the study's point of view and were also private moments. Other situations concerned private issues (e.g. health problems) of the participants or discussions on the details of forthcoming competitions. Nevertheless, such short interruptions in the recordings were not common in the study.

The advantages of using video technology in research, including observation, have been discussed by many authors (Knoblauch and Tuma 2011; Heath and Hindmarsh 2002; Hindmarsh and Heath 2007; Mondada 2008; Heath, Hindmarsh and Luff 2010) and for this reason they will be omitted in this book; however, it is important to stress its usability in observing the transmission of sports skills because it provides access to both talk and bodily comportment, 'which is considered necessary in order to explore the learners' knowings, tacit as well as explicit' (Nyberg 2014b).

Head-mounted cameras have several advantages that have been rarely discussed but that influenced their choice for this research project. First, they allow an 'extended first-person perspective' (Kindt 2011; Thain 2015; Waters, Waite and Frampton 2014). The wearable camera enables capturing the context of the subject's perspective as he/she moves through the world in relation to people, feelings and things. Moreover, the research participant has more control over what will be seen and heard (Schoonover, Kinsley and Spitler 2016). Second, the camera maintains an unbiased and naturalistic perspective by recording things as they emerge from the perspective of the actor (Pink 2015). It gives the possibility to look at interactions and communication in 'natural' settings. One should be aware that coaches can still adjust their behaviour while they are being observed during the training sessions by the researcher who is taking the notes (Frers 2009). However, the research participants' impressions that they shared at the end of the observation revealed that during the training course they forgot, at least most of the time, about the camera. Third, this kind of camera allows for observation of many details of the interactions between the coach and the learners, such as the relations between verbal communication and gestures, without the direct intervention of the researcher and interruption of the training sessions. It is also possible to precisely analyse whether and to what extent a coach's attention is focused on each participant. Fourth, some challenges and critical decisions that are present in video observations, such as the appropriate angle of the camera and zoom (Luff and Heath 2012), do not appear while using head-mounted cameras. This issue should be considered not only as a technical one but also as important from the point of view of constructing the data. And, fifth, convenience of use is an additional advantage of GoPro cameras, as one only has to turn it on and put it on the participant's head. Moreover, coaches and young athletes are used to being recorded during training sessions and competitions, and head-mounted cameras are becoming more popular in the field of sports.

One of the biggest advantages of a head-mounted camera is its 'invisibility'. During the training sessions, it was observed that with the passing of time the camera became, to a large extent, a 'natural', 'invisible' extension of the coach's body (Merleau-Ponty 2002[1948]). Therefore, one can speak of the 'camera's disappearance' during large portions of the training sessions, which should then contribute to the 'natural' character of the coaches' behaviour. However, it is important to note that the camera became visible in several situations that were similar in both France and in Poland. This happened mainly at the beginning of the training session, when the coaches put the camera on their head, which then aroused the children's interest. Additionally, during the recording the children sporadically came up close to the camera, asking questions about it, or saying something and waving to it. The coaches themselves also made the camera 'visible' by telling the children to 'watch out, the camera is watching you', 'don't forget, I am recording all of your behaviour', and so on. And, finally, the camera also appeared at the end of the training session, when some of the coaches asked the children to say goodbye to the camera. However, moments of this 'appearance' were much rarer than those of its disappearance.

3.5 Data analysis

A theoretical reading of the data (Kvale and Brinkmann 2009) was done, which means that the theoretical framework was applied in all of the data analysis. It was focused on tacit knowledge, which is transmitted to a large extent through non-verbal communication, and even if it is verbalised, it is understood only in a particular situation. All of the data were read and watched several times, although for the purpose of this publication, only those parts of the interviews and video recordings that concerned the transmission of practical knowledge were subjected to a detailed analysis.

The situated interviews, as mentioned above, were transcribed verbatim. Then their content was copied and split into five categories, related to the five parts of the interviews. The author of this book read the whole interviews to find information that would be significant to the problems studied here. This information was found mainly in two parts: the teaching methods and the (non)verbal communication. However, one could also find relevant data in other parts of the interviews, as illustrated by the issue of touch, which appeared during conversations regarding gender differences.

The analysis of the interviews had two phases. Its first aim was to find the main teaching methods that were being used by the coaches, and the second was to look for the limits of verbal transmission of knowledge and its explanation. As a consequence, each interview was coded twice: the first codes were related to the teaching methods as distinguished in the training sports manuals: verbal, based on demonstration, imaginative and practice. Two other categories were distinguished during this coding: use of visual materials and proxemics. During the second reading, the limits of the verbalisation of tacit knowledge were the focus; therefore, each fragment of the transcriptions in which this issue was raised, or indicated by the project investigators in the transcriptions (e.g. information that a coach had made a movement), were marked and subjected to a detailed analysis.

The analysis of apprenticeship was similar to that of the interviews and was based mainly on the researcher's notes, as well as on the impressions they shared after this phase of research. All of the field notes were read to find the main methods of teaching and the limits of verbal communication. This analysis was conducted second; therefore, the additional codes that emerged in the analysis of the interviews were used during its course. The quotations from the apprenticeship are marked AP, while those from the situated interviews are marked SI.

And, finally, a video interaction analysis (Knoblauch *et al.* 2006; Kissmann 2009; Knoblauch and Tuma 2011) was conducted. Quotations from these are marked VO and PL for the Polish observations and FR for the French observations. Additionally, the discipline and coach's gender are provided in all of the quotations. The process of analysis proposed by Knoblauch and Tuma (2011: 419) was used. In the first step of the analysis, each training session was watched and a chart with basic information, such as the time, 'topic' and remarks, was created for each session. These charts were made to be able to meander through all of the gathered material. After watching all of the videos, the decision to analyse only the main part of the training sessions was made because it is during this time of the training session that one can observe the largest number of interactions between the learner and the coach. Then a relevant action was chosen. A selected action can be called 'a teaching unit'. It is easy to indicate in the case of the training session – it starts with an explanation of a new exercise and ends when a coach announces the next exercise. Therefore, the selected action has its clear beginning and end. The 'teaching unit' also had a role as an 'analysis unit'; however, it was also divided into smaller parts, that is, explanation and practice.

A detailed analysis of the selected footage was conducted twice. First, all of the units were coded with reference to the teaching methods as distinguished in the sports coaching manuals. Second, a detailed analysis was conducted for each unit by taking into account the principle of sequentiality. To become familiar with the selected footage, its transcription, consisting of both verbal and non-verbal communication, was made. The aim of this analysis was to find patterns of communication in the process of knowledge transmission. It took into account both the similarities and the differences within and between the explored sports disciplines. In a majority of the cases, the author did not use the CA's standard of transcription (Jefferson 2004), because it did not seem appropriate for presentation of the data, which will be discussed in the last chapter.

During the analysis process, both intra-coder (Mackey and Gass 2005) and inter-coder reliability (Krippendorff 2004) were used. The principal investigator coded all of the data, and several weeks later she returned to the gathered data and re-coded a part of them. Then three of the project's investigators were asked to code two of the interviews each. The analysis of the video data was discussed during data sessions (Heath *et al.* 2010; Hindmarsh and Tutt 2012) with the participation of the principal investigator and four of the research team members. Additionally, during the analysis process of the data, the principal investigator used the investigators' field notes from the observations. Is should also be stressed that the same codes appeared useful in the case of the interview transcriptions, field notes from the apprenticeship and video recording transcriptions.

Therefore, in this study, three forms of triangulation were used during the process of data gathering and data analysis: (1) data triangulation, (2) investigator triangulation and (3) methodological triangulation (Denzin 1978). The data were gathered across the sports disciplines in two countries by six researchers with the use of three different researcher methods. All of the investigators, beyond conducting the research tasks, consulted the research tools and coded a small part of the gathered data in order to enhance the research study's validity and reliability.

References

Andrieu, B., Paintendre, A. and Burel, N. (eds.), 2014, *Enseigner par son corps* [*Learning through Own Body*], L'Harmattan, Paris.
Bourdieu, P., 1977, *Outline of a Theory of Practice*, Cambridge University Press, Cambridge.

Carlgren, I., 2007, 'The content of schooling: From knowledge and subject matter to knowledge formation and subject specific ways of knowing', in E. Forsberg (ed.), *Curriculum Theory Revisited, Studies in Educational Policy and Educational Philosophy*, pp. 81–96, Uppsala University, Uppsala.

Denzin, N.K., 1978, *The Research Act: A Theoretical Introduction to Sociological Methods* (2nd ed.), McGraw-Hill, New York.

Downey, G., Dalidowicz, M. and Manson, P.H., 2015, 'Apprenticeship as method: Embodied learning in ethnographic practice', *Qualitative Research*, 15(2), 183–200.

Faure, S., 2000, *Apprendre par corps. Socio-anthropologie des techniques de danse* [*Learning through the Body: Socio-Anthropology of the Dance Techniques*], La Dispute, Paris.

Frers, L., 2009, 'Video research in the open: Encounters involving the researcher-camera', in U.T. Kissmann (ed.), *Video Interaction Analysis: Methods and Methodology*, pp. 155–177, Peter Lang, Frankfurt am Main.

Gieser, T., 2008, 'Embodiment, emotion and empathy: A phenomenological approach to apprenticeship learning', *Anthropological Theory*, 8, 299–318.

Heath, Ch. and Hindmarsh, J., 2002, 'Analysing interaction: Video, ethnography and situated conduct', in T. May (ed.), *Qualitative Research in Action*, pp. 99–121, SAGE Publications Ltd., London.

Heath, Ch., Hindmarsh, J. and Luff, P., 2010, *Video in Qualitative Research*, SAGE Publications Ltd., London.

Hindmarsh, J. and Heath, C., 2007, 'Video-based studies of work practice', *Sociology Compass*, 1(1), 156–173.

Hindmarsh, J. and Tutt, D., 2012, 'Video in analytic practice', in S. Pink (ed.), *Advances in Visual Methodology*, pp. 57–73, SAGE Publications Ltd., London.

Ingold, T., 2000, *The Perception of the Environment: Essays on Livelihood, Dwelling and Skill*, Routledge, London.

Jakubowska, H., 2014, *Gra ciałem. Praktyki i dyskursy różnicowania płci w sporcie* [*The Game of the Body: The Practices and Discourses of Gender Differentiation in Sport*], Wydawnictwo Naukowe PWN, Warszawa.

Janik, A., 1996, *Kunskapsbegrepp i praktisk filosofi* [*Concept of Knowledge in Philosophy of Practice*], Brutus Östlings Bokförlag Symposion, Skåne län.

Jefferson, G., 2004, 'Glossary of transcript symbols with an introduction', in G.H. Lerner (ed.), *Conversation Analysis: Studies from the First Generation*, pp. 13–31, John Benjamins, Amsterdam.

Kindt, D., 2011, 'Seeing through the eyes of the students: First impressions of recording in the classroom with a GoPro® head-mounted camcorder', *Journal of the School of Contemporary International Studies*, 7, 179–199.

Kissmann, U.T. (ed.), 2009, *Video Interaction Analysis: Methods and Methodology*, Peter Lang, Frankfurt am Main.

Knoblauch, H., Schnettler, B., Raab, J. and Soeffner, H.G., 2006, *Video Analysis: Methodology and Methods: Qualitative Audiovisual Data Analysis in Sociology*, Peter Lang, Frankfurt am Main.

Knoblauch, H. and Tuma, R., 2011, 'Videography: An interpretative approach to video-recorded micro-social interaction', in E. Margolis and L. Pauwels (eds.),

The SAGE Handbook of Visual Research Methods, pp. 414–430, SAGE Publications Ltd, London.

Krippendorff, K., 2004, *Content Analysis: An Introduction to Its Methodology* (2nd ed.), SAGE Publications Ltd, Thousand Oaks, CA.

Kvale, S. and Brinkmann, S., 2009, *Interviews: Learning the Craft of Qualitative Research Interviewing*, Sage, Los Angeles.

Luff, P. and Heath, Ch., 2012, 'Some "technical challenges" of video analysis: Social actions, objects, material realities and the problems of perspective', *Qualitative Research*, 12(3), 255–279.

Mackey, A. and Gass, S.M., 2005, *Second Language Research: Methodology and Design*, Lawrence Erlbaum Associates. Mahwah, NJ.

Magill, R.A., 2011, *Motor Learning and Control: Concepts and Applications*, McGraw-Hill, New York.

Mauss, M., 1973[1935], 'Techniques of the body', *Economy and Society*, 2(1), 70–88.

McDonagh, E. and Pappano, L., 2008, *Playing with the Boys: Why Separate Is Not Equal in Sports*, Oxford University Press, New York.

Merleau-Ponty, M., 2002[1948], *Phenomenology of Perception*, Routledge, London.

Mondada, L., 2008, 'Using Video for a Sequential and Multimodal Analysis of Social Interaction: Videotaping Institutional Telephone Calls', *Forum Qualitative Sozialforschung/Forum: Qualitative Social Research*, 9(3). Viewed 7 November 2016 from www.qualitative-research.net/index.php/fqs/article/view/1161

Nyberg, G., 2014b, 'Exploring "knowings" in human movement: The practical knowledge of pole-vaulters', *European Physical Education Review*, 20(1), 72–89.

Pink, S., 2009, *Doing Sensory Ethnography*, SAGE Publications Ltd., London.

Pink, S., 2015, 'Going Forward Through the World: Thinking Theoretically about First Person Perspective Digital Ethnography', *Integrative Psychological and Behavioral Science*, 49(2), 239–252.

Polanyi, M., 1966, *The Tacit Dimension*, University of Chicago Press, Chicago.

Schoonover, D., Kinsley, K.M. and Spitler, J., 2016, 'GoPro as an ethnographic tool: A wayfinding study in an academic library', *Journal of Access Services*, 13(1), 7–23.

Sperschneider, W., 2007, 'Video ethnography under industrial constraints: Observational techniques and video analysis', in S. Pink (ed.), *Visual Interventions: Applied Visual Anthropology*, pp. 273–294, Berghahn Books, New York.

Standal, Ø.F. and Engelsrud, G., 2013, 'Researching embodiment in movement contexts: A phenomenological approach', *Sport, Education and Society*, 18(2), 154–166.

Thain, A., 2015, 'A bird's-eye view of Leviathan', *Visual Anthropology Review*, 31(1), 41–48.

Waters, P., Waite, S. and Frampton, I., 2014, 'Play frames, or framed play? The use of film cameras in visual ethnographic research with children', *Journal of Playwork Practice*, 1(1), 23–38.

Ylirisku, S.P. and Buur, J., 2007, *Designing with Video: Focusing the User-Centred Design Process*, Springer-Verlag, London.

Young, I.M., 1990, *Throwing Like a Girl, and Other Essays in Feminist Philosophy and Social Theory*, University of Indiana Press, Bloomington.

4 Transmission of tacit knowledge

4.1 Course of the training sessions

All of the observed training sessions started with a warm-up. This part lasted, on average, about ten minutes. Its content depended mainly on the sports discipline, the learners' ages and their sports level. At the beginning of the judo training sessions for the youngest learners, the coaches mainly organised games (e.g. tag or dodgeball) and asked the learners to do some simple exercises (e.g. jumping jacks, arm circling, hip rotations). The same activities were also usually done at the end of each training session. In the case of athletics, only one coach organised a game at the beginning of the training sessions (another at the end), and no games were observed in swimming. The older judo apprentices started the training sessions with a set of body conditioning exercises with elements of judo. These were performed individually or in pairs.

The athletics training sessions usually started with running around the stadium or a gymnasium and continued with numerous exercises, such as skips, arm circling, swings, and so on. The learners practised individually, one after the other, in one or two rows. One can distinguish two kinds of warm-ups in swimming: outside the water and in the water. The former were observed during four of the thirteen training sessions, whereas most of the warm-ups took place in the water. The learners were asked to swim two, four or eight (in the case of a short swimming pool) laps in any style they wanted to. The warm-ups were conducted by the coaches in all of the three analysed sports disciplines. Only in one case (in athletics) was one of the learners asked to lead this part of the training session.

After the warm-ups, the main part of the training sessions began. This part was focused on learning new techniques and/or improving techniques that the learners had already been taught. Once again, differences could be observed, depending on the sports discipline, age and sports level. The judo training sessions were quite similar, with two exceptions, in the youngest group and in the most advanced group. Usually, one could observe the following sequence of activities:

1   a demonstration with verbal explanation of a technique given by the coach with one of the learners,
2   practising in pairs, during which the coach would intervene in different ways,
3   change of pairs (observed in some training sessions),
4   demonstration of another technique.

Most often the groups practised a few techniques (e.g. throws, holds) during one training session. The number of techniques was smaller among younger learners and larger in the case of the oldest ones. During training sessions with the youngest group (7–9 years old), the coach did not present any technique, and the course consisted of games, simple exercises and fights, whereas in the most advanced group, called 'Talents', demonstration was very limited. Besides the exercises, the coaches organised short fights between the learners. These usually took place at the end of the training sessions. One could also observe that the coaches used different kinds of 'punishment' (e.g. jumping jacks or squats) with the learners, without regard to their age. The punishment concerned the whole group if some of its members reacted too slowly to the coach's commands or did not listen to him/her carefully, but also the pair that had finished a particular exercise last.

The athletics training sessions were much more differentiated, which results, in part, from the diversification of this sports discipline. Some training sessions were focused on a particular competition, such as javelin throw, pole vault or hurdles, while others had a more general character. Additionally, some of the training sessions were conducted in stadiums and others in sports halls. One could also observe a large difference in the number of training participants, from three to seventeen persons. As compared to judo, demonstration was more rare and was mainly observed during exercises with sports equipment, such as a pole or javelin. During the main part of the training sessions, the learners were asked to exercise several techniques or one technique and its variations. Examples of these are the starts for a race, the throwing of a ball (in the case of younger children), javelin throw and hurdling. For the younger age groups, the exercises had a more body-conditioning character, and for the older, they were more often focused on a specific technique. The coaches sometimes organised races or competitions of throwing among the learners who had been divided into two groups (both same-gender and mixed).

In contrast, the swimming training sessions were similar to one another. After warm-up, the coaches gave a command to complete an indicated number of laps (from two to eight) in a specific style. During the training course, fins and swimming foams were often used and, in one case in France, also pool pipes. In the case of less-advanced groups, one could observe more demonstration accompanying the commands, while in the case of more advanced groups, demonstration was limited. When the apprentices were practising, the coaches reprimanded them, gave additional advice and presented the correct movement, which will be discussed later. However, in the more advanced groups, they did not follow all of the exercises, which has also been observed in other sports training sessions. In swimming, when the learners had finished performing one task, the coach gave the next command. Each of the observed coaches was outside the water during the whole training course.

Almost all of the training sessions, regardless of the discipline, finished with a cool-down consisting of loosening and/or relaxation exercises. Some individual and common games were organised in the case of the youngest groups. For example, in one group the coach did one throw with each child; in another the children had rope-climbing at the end of the training session. These activities were perceived as a kind of 'reward' for the learners' good behaviour. There is also another case that is worth mentioning as two groups (observed at the same swimming pool) finished their training by doing exercises related to safety in the water. The children had to jump into the water in their 'normal' clothes, including their shoes, and then swim to reach the swimming pool's edge.

Usually the training sessions had the same content for the whole group; however, in a few cases some exceptions could be observed. The coaches assigned different exercises to either one person or to several when a group member or members

1   had significantly different sports levels, either lower or higher than the majority of the group (athletics in France)
2   were much younger and as a result were smaller than the rest (athletics and judo in Poland)
3   were not in fact a group member but practised with the same coach during the training session (judo in Poland).

These differences were not observed during the swimming training sessions, which were homogeneous according to the criteria of age and sports level. Also, twice (in athletics) a few learners had arrived late to the training session and, as a consequence, the coaches repeated the same training course for these latecomers.

Most often the training sessions were conducted by one coach, although some exceptions can been noted. During one athletics training session in Poland, there were two female coaches (the main coach and her assistant); the same was observed twice in France in swimming (one time there were two women, and one time a man was the main coach and a woman was his assistant). In judo, during one training session in France, there were even three coaches who all had clear roles; one was responsible for training, and the other two supported him. Additionally, in swimming and once in athletics, the investigators observed training sessions during which a warm-up was conducted by one coach and afterwards the group was divided into smaller groups that worked with different coaches. In all of these cases, only one coach was observed.

Therefore, each training session consisted of three parts: a warm-up, the main part and a cool-down. From the point of view of an external observer, the process of knowledge transmission and sports technique transfer is the most visible in the main part of the training sessions, during which participants learn new or develop already-known techniques and skills. It is also that part of the training session when one can see much more direct interactions between the coaches and the learners (both verbal and non-verbal). The coaches not only demonstrate a particular movement but also correct the learners' movement, while during the other parts of the training sessions, they pay significantly less attention to the way the learners perform the exercises. Therefore, the detailed analysis was focused on the main part of the training sessions and the ways of teaching that were used during its course. However, it should be emphasised that the acquisition of tacit (sports) knowledge takes place all the time. During the interviews the coaches indicated that, for example, during the games, they also teach children to learn some skills, even without the children being aware of this:

> We invent some games and they [the children] do not even know that they are practising judo.
>
> (judo, W1, SI)

> It is known that we use some forms of games in the initial stage of training. We do this until the eighth training session. These concern entering the water, moving in the water, opening the eyes under the water, swimming, diving, etc. One has to teach these things in the form of a game to make it interesting to the child, but also to have measurable effects of this work with children.
>
> (swimming, M1, SI)

> It is also a way of hiding knowledge transfer. Sometimes the children think that we are just playing and they do not know when they are learning, e.g. rolls forward, so due to this they also learn judo throws. So for them it is a game, and for me it is an element with which they learn.
>
> (judo, W2, SI)

Then I tell them 'Now we swim and tickle ourselves under the arm with our thumb'. I demonstrate this movement and this way they perform the correct movement of the elbow fold. And they grasp it because it is funny, they are tickling themselves and others. It is an easy exercise to conduct which shows the whole 'philosophy' of this fold.

(swimming, W1, SI)

Similarly, the fights between participants during training sessions in judo should be seen as an element of the teaching process. As one coach stated:

'Look at how the other persons fight because you will also learn from this'.

(VO, PL, judo2, M)

This process of knowledge transmission remains less visible to an external observer, but the fighting should still be seen as knowledge acquisition, that is, its embodiment in practice. Therefore this topic will remain on the margins of this book. In the case of games, however, knowledge transmission is difficult to see for a researcher who does not have sports experience as an athlete or as a coach. However, it would be interesting and worth analysing together with the coaches those parts of the training sessions during which the children had different games by presenting the coaches the video recordings and asking them to reveal their ways of knowledge transmission.

4.2   How is tacit knowledge transmitted?

Both verbal and non-verbal communication are inextricably linked in the process of sports knowledge transmission. On the one hand, one is not able to explicate everything only with words (speech), but, on the other, demonstration (or drawing in the case of manuals) is not sufficient in many situations. As was revealed by Schindler's (2009) experiment conducted during video data analysis, neither exclusively verbal information nor exclusively visual information allows one to 'see' the process of sports skills transfer.

Polish sports manuals related to swimming, judo and athletics distinguish four main methods of knowledge transmission used during sports training sessions:

1   verbal communication
   a)   limited to the name of an action
   b)   explanation of movement

2   demonstration (in swimming, in the water and outside the water), including the use of video recordings

3 imaginative methods (e.g. exercises in thought, use of metaphors, fights
   against an imaginary opponent)
4 practical action

(Wiesner 1999; Karpiński 2001; Kuźmicki 2011)

The study conducted here revealed that the use of video recordings should be distinguished from demonstration. Demonstration, which can be understood in the Goffmanian way as 'performances of a task like activity out of its usual functional context' (Goffman 1974: 79), was very common during the training sessions. Its main aim was to present a particular movement or course of action. The use of video materials was quite rare among the analysed age groups. Additionally, the principal investigator decided to distinguish proxemics as a separate teaching method. Although the listed methods of knowledge transmission very often appeared simultaneously, they will be discussed separately for the purpose of this analysis.

4.2.1 Verbal communication

The coaches indicated demonstration and explanation as the main methods used during the training sessions. Answers to questions posed during the situated interviews were very similar within and across the sports disciplines. Their analysis, as well as the analysis of the video recordings, shows that the coaches' utterances occur in three main forms: (1) the name of a particular movement, exercise or technique, (2) the explanation of a movement, and (3) the indication of mistakes.

The first form of verbal communication was observed mainly during the warm-ups and training sessions that had a more general, physical conditioning character, when the coaches listed successive exercises that should be done by the learners. In the youngest groups, mainly in athletics, these utterances were usually supported by demonstration. For example, a Polish coach asked the children to do leaps and showed them how to should do them (e.g. lift the left hand and the right leg, then vice versa); a French coach asked the children to lift their knees while simultaneously demonstrating this movement. In other groups, the coaches used only verbal commands. For example, they said 'now forward roll' (VO, PL, judo2, W) or 'turn facing the centre and make lateral steps without crossing the legs' (VO, FR, judo1, M).

Apart from the first phase of the training sessions, the use of utterances exclusively was observed in the most advanced groups, mainly in swimming and, to a smaller extent, in judo. A significant part of these training sessions was focused on skills improvement; the learners already had theoretical knowledge as to how to perform a particular technique ('theoretical knowledge how'), so naming it (e.g. the swimming style) was a sufficient indication. Examples of such utterances include the following:

> OK. Listen, the main task. Eight times, 25 metres. You start as quickly as possible. Thirty seconds. Then we put in fins and swim the crawl for 300 metres. Four minutes. We relax during the crawl.
>
> (VO, PL, swimming1, M)

> Now we have one more task. You try to swim the crawl across the whole pool as quickly as possible and take as few breaths as possible.
>
> (VO, PL, swimming8, M)

> OK. Now we have four times, 50 metres in four styles, 25 metres fast and 25 metres slow. During the fast 25 metres, the first 15 are maximal frequency and the next 10 are mini-cycles.
>
> (VO, FR, swimming4, M)

The judo coaches used only verbal messages when working with the most advanced groups, naming an activity if the exercise was already known, such as a roll or a hold. This can be illustrated by an example from France, in which the coach commanded, 'Now a front roll, right and left' (VO, FR, judo4, M), and by the case of a Polish judo training session during which the coach said to the participants,

> Now, one person is lying on their stomach, and we recall all the techniques to make a hold. I demonstrated to you once the possibilities we have, and now we will try to think about what we can do.
>
> (VO, PL, judo5, M)

The observed differences can be explained by the distinction between 'theoretical' and 'practical knowledge how' (Gascoigne and Thornton 2013). Children who start practising a particular sport have neither 'theoretical' nor 'practical knowledge how'; therefore, they need a demonstration of the movements because the names of the actions are insufficient for them to know what to do. By gaining experience the learners will gain 'theoretical knowledge how'; they will know what they should do when they hear the name of a particular exercise or technique. With time they will also acquire practical knowledge, and they will be able to use their skills in sports competitions.

During the main part of the training sessions, verbal communication was used primarily to explain a movement. This almost always occurred together with a demonstration, as the coaches answered the question as to which teaching methods should be used:

I always show and explain at the same time. For example, first I put my turned right foot forward, and I say, 'I put my turned right foot forward'.

(judo W1, SI)

Without a doubt demonstration. Of course, verbally it means explanation.

(athletics, W2, SI)

First, it is rather an explanation and a demonstration. It also depends on the type of exercise.

(athletics, W3, SI)

The indissolubility of demonstration and explanation was confirmed during the observations, as it was nearly impossible to observe solely verbal communication in the explanation of a movement. Therefore, one should speak about verbal guidance within a demonstration (Schindler 2009) rather than solely explanation. The same can be stated about the third form of utterances: indication of mistakes. In this case words were very often complemented by gestures, or the gestures and motions were supported by words.

However, in order to correct the learners' movements, the coach sometimes used solely verbal communication. One can distinguish between two main practices in this context. First, the coaches named only the part of the body that was in an incorrect position or that had made a wrong movement. This was very common during the training sessions and can be illustrated by numerous Polish and French examples from all three disciplines. One could hear the coaches saying only the word: 'knee', 'head', 'arms', 'hips', 'left foot', and so on. Sometimes, by adding a verb or an adverb to the name of the body part, the coach indicated how its movement or position should be changed. Examples of these are: 'legs wide', 'hide the head', 'pull the knee up high', 'arm extended'. This use of verbal practices was also observed by Faure (1999). These utterances represent very well the form of tacit knowledge that is verbalised; it can be understood only when someone is practising and the coach gives her/him a hint. When one extracts the sentence from a particular context, it becomes incomprehensible and useless.

Second, in order to correct a way of performing the exercises, the coaches used, although much more rarely, longer utterances without demonstration or correction of the learner's body. Examples of these include the following:

We remember that we have to insert a knee clearly and deeply. Of course, we try to catch the head, grip it so that the partner cannot move.

(VO, PL, judo5, M)

S. [the boy's name], do not stop your leg movement when you have your arms under the water. They should be working all the time.

(VO, PL, swimming1, M)

[After a long jump] H. [the boy's name], when I tell you that you have to speed up, to be more precise, I want your legs to move faster on the ground. Do you understand what I mean? Try to move faster, OK?

(VO, FR, athletics2, M)

This was also observed during the researchers' apprenticeship. One of them wrote in his field notes after an athletics training session:

Afterwards, I did this exercise myself. She [the coach] corrected me only verbally. She did not touch me. At this moment, commands such as 'please straighten the leg back more', 'your leg in the front should be stronger' appeared.

(AP, athletics, W2)

These utterances can be perceived as coaching rules or 'hints' (Collins 2010) that help the learner perform a particular action the way it should be done. As was mentioned earlier, these verbalisations were usually supported by the coaches' gestures and demonstration. In smaller groups the coaches gave these utterances to each participant individually after his/her performance, as observed, for example, in France during a long jump training session and in Poland during a pole vault training session. In the larger groups, the 'hints' were usually addressed to the whole group or to selected members. One can refer to two kinds of reflection when analysing the coaches' remarks given just after the athletes' performance. These are reflection-in-action and reflection-on-action (Schön 1991). An athlete discussing an action with a coach explains his/her reflection-in-action, and by doing this she/he reflects on action (Nyberg 2014b).

Utterances used during the training sessions can be divided according to their functions and complexity, as presented above. They can also be categorised in different ways. Faure (1999), in her research of dance, indicated that verbal utterances refer to (1) directions and positions, (2) action categories (lifting, folding, etc.) and (3) names of footsteps. On the basis of the analysis of the gathered video data it was also possible to distinguish three main categories of the coaches' statements. First, these concerned, similarly to Faure's study, actions. The coaches used a verb to indicate what should be done, such as 'hold', 'lift' or 'lean down'. Second, they 'situated' the body in space and described the spatial position of the body and its parts by using expressions such as 'closer' ('stand closer to the hurdle' in athletics, 'come closer to your partner' in judo), 'higher' (e.g. 'take off high' in athletics; 'the right hand high' in judo) and 'lower' (e.g. 'head lower' in swimming). And, third, they indicated the way of performing an action, which was often related to the force or tension that should to be used. These expressions were very common:

- 'strong' (e.g. 'belly and legs strong' in swimming, 'we hold on strong' in judo, 'and strong up' in athletics)
- 'deep' (e.g. 'we have to put the knee/leg in deep' in judo and athletics)
- 'loose' (e.g. throw or run 'loose')

An analysis of the utterances would not be complete without taking into account the linguistic and paralinguistic tools that were used in the coaches' verbal communication. Based on the video recordings of the training sessions, four of these were identified: change of voice tone, specific accentuation, word repetition and onomatopoeias. Some of these tools were used to highlight the importance of a particular movement or the role of a particular part of the body. For example, the coaches extended the words by dividing them into syllables (which is more visible in the Polish language than in its English translation). Another observed practice was the repetition of a single word that was the name of a part of the body or of an action. Also, a change in voice tone was observed. It appeared mainly in two contexts. First, during the training sessions with the youngest children, the coaches used a gentler voice and many diminutives. Second, individual coaches working with the most advanced group had a severe tone of voice when they shouted out different remarks to the swimming learners. However, these shouts could also have resulted from the noise that is specific to a swimming pool. This can be illustrated by the example of a French female swimming coach who wanted to give some remarks to one girl. When she started calling the girl's name using a 'normal' voice, the girl did not hear her. The coach started to wave, but the girl continued to swim. Finally, only shouting turned out to be effective. The coaches also used onomatopoeias – words that phonetically imitated the sound that was being described. Some of them, instead of determining the pace with the use of words, clapped and counted out to indicate the appropriate pace (Table 4.1).

The movement's pace was also indicated by the Polish word 'hop!' (usually used as a synonym for 'jump!'). Its use reveals that a single word plays a different role during sports training sessions, as during the observed training sessions this word was used in several different ways: as a pace-maker (mainly in athletics), as an alternative to a whistle to start a lap or run (swimming and athletics) and to indicate an important moment in the

Table 4.1 Linguistic and paralinguistic tools used in the coaches' verbal communication

---

Extended words
- *a hand is clen:ched:* [in Polish: *za:ci:śnię:ta*] (VO, PL, judo1, W)
- *M.* [the boy's name], *legs, legs* [in Polish: *nogi, no:gi*] (VO, PL, swimming1, M)
- *Stretch out your hand far a:way* [in Polish: *da:le:ko*] (VO, PL, swimming6, M)

Word repetition
- *(. . .) legs, legs, legs* (VO, PL, swimming2, W)
- *I run, run, run, loosely, loosely, loosely* (VO, PL, judo8, W)
- *We keep, keep, keep pace to not make the breaks too long* (VO, PL, athletics8, M)
- *The arms, arms, arms. Gently, gently, gently. Raise them, raise, raise* (VO, FR, athletics1, M)
- [a javelin] *Up, up* (VO, FR, athletics3, M)
- *Do not move, do not move* (VO, FR, swimming1, W)

Change of tone of voice
- *One movement to a breaststroke, one. ONE MOVEMENT* (VO, FR, swimming1, W)
- *HIPS! BUTTOCKS UNDER THE WATER* (VO, PL, swimming6, M)
- *S.* [the boy's name], *ARM OUTSTRETCHED* (VO, FR, athletics3, M)

Onomatopoeias
- *And dynamically, pach, pach* [an onomatopoeic word in Polish that denotes the dynamic rhythm of leg movement], *the legs are moving, go on* (VO, PL, athletics3, M)
- *At the end one has to pull in* [the coach says 'pull in' a distinct way which gives the impression of much effort] *here, strongly* (VO, PL, athletics3, M)

Pace determined by counting or clapping
- *and C skip in the pace that I clap* (VO, PL, athletics5, W)
- *we will try to throw* [a javelin] *normally. One, two, one, two* [when saying 'one, two' the coach makes steps] *and we throw* (VO, FR, athletics3, M)

---

whole movement. For example, the judo coaches repeated 'hop, hop, hop' to impose the pace of the movements, while the swimming coach also repeated this word to make the learners pay attention to the wrong pace of their head movements. During verbal guidance within the demonstration, the judo coaches also used the word 'hop' to indicate some moments in the 'fighting episodes', such as when one should draw an opponent in and throw him/her.

The different examples that have been presented here reveal that tacit knowledge, even if it is verbalised, is usually situation-dependent. The use of words such as 'hop', 'legs' or 'head' cannot be understood outside the particular situation when they were said; therefore, it would be incorrect to recognise all of verbalised communication as situation-independent.

Moreover, a part of the knowledge is perceived as very difficult and even impossible to explain verbally. During the interviews the coaches were asked to finish the following sentence: 'In words, the most difficult to explain is. . .'. Their answers can be divided into three main categories. First, they indicated a given technique or technical exercises:

> Technique. One has to demonstrate it. It is not possible to explain a throw or how to hold without demonstration.
>
> (judo, W1, SI)

> Technical exercises, [such as] the throw of a rubber ball. It is easier to demonstrate it, how the arm and hips should move. All of these things are easier to show than to explain verbally.
>
> (athletics, M1, SI)

Second, they indicated some exercises in their discipline, such as vault jump or a cartwheel:

> Gymnastics, one has to demonstrate it. Jump vault with legs apart – a piece of cake. But if they don't see it, they will not know [how to do it]. One cannot say to them: optimal run-up, not too fast, jump on both legs, arms' position, etc. They do not see this. Gymnastics. Cartwheel. They have to see it.
>
> (athletics, M2, SI)

And, third, the coaches stated that all sports knowledge is difficult to express verbally:

> Exercises or, more generally, movement.
>
> (athletics, W3, SI)

> I don't know. In swimming, it is better to demonstrate it. It is better to demonstrate everything.
>
> (swimming, M3, SI)

The limits of verbal communication were indicated by the coaches but also observed in their behaviour during the interviews. When answering the questions, from time to time they made a gesture or performed a movement to demonstrate a technique or the position of a particular part of the body. This was observed in all of the analysed sports disciplines. One can distinguish two main contexts in which the coaches completed their statements with non-verbal communication. First, the coaches used both single gestures and more complex displays when they answered the question as to what is the most difficult to learn. The judo coaches indicated some actions, such as rolls (e.g. zempo-ukemi) or throws (e.g. o-soto-gari), and demonstrated them. In the case of throws, the display was made without an opponent. The athletics and swimming coaches, when answering the same question, also added to their answers a demonstration of some of the movements and body-part positions in running hurdles and the breaststroke or crawl:

> R: Which exercise elements are the most difficult to explain? C: Hurdles are hard to explain, because it is [the coach starts to demonstrate a movement] (. . .).
>
> (athletics, M2, SI)

> The hand and leg movements are difficult because it is not easy [saying this, the coach bends her hand and tightens particular muscles of her forearm]. One has to bend here and take a breath at the appropriate moment. [We teach that] the arms move separately, the legs separately. It is difficult to teach a breaststroke.
>
> (swimming, W1, SI)

> For example, in the crawl, setting the foot in the position where the toes are stretched to the outside [the coach demonstrates an incorrect position of the feet], and we would like people to do it this way [the coach demonstrates the correct position of the feet].
>
> (swimming, M3, SI)

However, it should be noted that in three cases (twice in judo and once in athletics), the idea to demonstrate a movement could have been, in some way, caused by the researchers' additional questions. The coaches' words were not clear enough to the researchers, and they asked for more explanation. While explaining, the coaches started to demonstrate:

> C: For example one of the main techniques is zempo-ukemi. It is a forward roll over the shoulder.
> R: Over the shoulder?
> C: Forward, over the shoulder [saying this the coach demonstrates the movement in the air].
>
> (judo, M3, SI)

> R: Have you noticed that there is a problem in explaining something verbally that recurs all the time?
> C: Yes, high knee skips. An easy exercise.
> R: High knee skips? Which means?

C: [The coach demonstrates]. It is an exercise where one leg is bent up, and the second is straight.

(athletics, W2, SI)

The second main context in which the coaches used demonstration during the interviews was to show either correct or incorrect movement of the body or its parts, such as hands, arms or legs. This was observed mainly in athletics and swimming:

A step is shaped through exercises and paces. It is important to have a slack in the arms. The arms have to help us, not disturb, not brake; the arms' movement is very important. Working this way [the coach demonstrates incorrect movement], you brake. Working this way [the coach demonstrates correct movement, with the arms closer to the body], you help yourself, because you accelerate additionally. This has significant meaning.

(athletics, W1, SI)

It should also be mentioned that one coach used the learner's body as a tool to make a demonstration during the interview:

You ask me how I correct mistakes? I will show you how. [command to one boy] Make a few circles. When I see that it is wrong, I take a leg [the coach touches the learner's leg], and I go [he makes the movement of the boy's leg in the correct way], and then I let him go.

(athletics, M2, SI)

The interviews revealed that an utterance is not always an effective tool for transferring sports skills or for explaining the transmission process. Although sports coaches can be perceived as experts of tacit knowledge, that is, people who not only see the details of sports techniques and teach them but are also able to articulate their knowledge (Carlgren 2007; Magill 2011), they can have difficulties in verbalising all of the aspects of embodied knowledge in sport. Therefore, it is not surprising that one can observe the common use of demonstration in the process of transmitting tacit knowledge.

4.2.2 Demonstration

Demonstration, as was already mentioned, is one of the two main methods of knowledge transmission, besides explanation. This was emphasised by all of the coaches during the interviews. The judo coaches stated the following:

There is always something to demonstrate.

(judo M1, SI)

We mainly make demonstration. Judo is not an easy sport; therefore, we are standing all the time on the mat, and we have to demonstrate the techniques, and we explain.

(judo K1, SI)

The athletics coaches also assumed that demonstration joined with explanation is the most effective method of teaching:

Without a doubt, demonstration. Of course, verbally it means explanation. I also try to use athletes who are at the stadium.

(athletics, W2, SI)

It has to be demonstration; it will not work any other way.

(athletics, W3, SI)

It has to be demonstration; the child has to see the movement.

(athletics, M2, SI)

The swimming training sessions were also based on demonstration and subsequent explanation:

Demonstration is most important to me because they [the children] can see what the movement should look like. [For example,] I show them that they should turn the hand this way, here [the coach shows the movement]. I think that one has to talk less and mainly demonstrate.

(swimming, W1, SI)

As regards teaching methods for children, it has to be demonstration and explanation. Without this, there is no chance that the child will understand it. One has to demonstrate several times.

(swimming, M1, SI)

The swimming coaches noticed that demonstration is important not only because embodied tacit knowledge is difficult to transfer verbally but also because of the age of the learners and their lack of experience:

The choice of method depends on who you're teaching. At the higher level, the demonstrative methods are nearly absent. It is also said that when somebody has been swimming for a long time, he/she understands the jargon.

(swimming, W2, SI)

They also noticed absent-mindedness related to the age of the learners:

> I explain five times, describe, embellish, explain everything, and they are watching me, listen for only five minutes and do not know how to swim.
> (swimming, W1, SI)

> The children, they are very often absent-minded, very often lose the thread. As a consequence, the teacher, coach or instructor has to repeat something several times. And they have to demonstrate it several times.
> (swimming, M1, SI)

These answers were confirmed by the video-based observations. Demonstration was used during all of the training sessions; however, each had a very different course. The coach displayed the whole movement, a part of it or movement of a particular part of the body (e.g. the hands), and or just made single gestures. The two main aims of the demonstration were to (1) display a new task (exercise) and (2) present mistakes that were made, such as in judo, how a particular throw or hold should not be made or in swimming, wrong arm movements. As for the differences between the analysed disciplines, the use of demonstration in each of them will be presented separately.

4.2.2.1 Judo

In judo, the main part of the training sessions consisted of several units that were easy to distinguish. In most of the cases, the coaches started with a demonstration of a judo technique, such as a particular throw or hold. These can be perceived as the 'fighting episodes', or the 'chains of movements that simulate what could be a moment within a fight' (Schindler 2009: 144). The demonstration was usually made by the coach him/herself, by the coach with one of the learners, or, least frequently, by a pair of learners. Therefore, one can say that within this method of knowledge transmission the coaches used the learners' bodies 'as a means to demonstrate an episode' (Schindler 2009: 145), which resulted mainly from the fact that judo is a contact sport and, as such, is practised in pairs.

It should be noted that with the exception of two groups (one consisted only of girls and the other of the youngest children), only boys were chosen to take part in the demonstrations. One could suppose that this resulted from physiological differences; however, this was also observed in those groups where at least one girl was older and bigger than her peers. Even if the coach chose the smallest participant, it was always also a boy. The reasons for these choices could have been perception of gender differences, higher level of boys' skills or concern regarding the 'touch issue', which will be discussed later. The data gathered here do not allow to formulate a clear answer; however, this issue is worth taking up in further studies.

During the research team members' apprenticeship, the coaches made the demonstrations themselves (without an opponent) and/or asked one of the training session participants to help them to present a throw:

> First, the coach demonstrated (on a 'virtual' opponent) what it should look like and then asked one female athlete to come up to make possible a full demonstration of the shoulder throw.
>
> (AP, judo, M3)

In this stage of the study, it was also common that the coaches first demonstrated a throw alone and then together with the researcher:

> The female coach asked me to come closer and started talking about particular movements and at the same time demonstrated these movements with her own body. Next she continued to describe how they should be done and at the same time demonstrated them on my body.
>
> (AP, judo, W1)

Despite the common use of demonstration during the sports training sessions, some differences were observed with reference to the learners' age and sports level. In the case of the youngest children's groups, demonstrations were quite rare because the children had not yet been taught any judo techniques. The aim of their training sessions was to contribute to their sports development and to provide healthy activities rather than to teach particular advanced sports skills. In the slightly older groups, the demonstrations were more frequent and even pertained to simple movements and exercises. Therefore, it is possible to indicate the age boundary at which it becomes important not only that the children do certain sports exercises but when the way to perform them should be shown. That is why children receive both an explanation and a demonstration to be able to imitate the correct movement. At the end of the continuum, one can find the oldest and most advanced groups (which were observed only in Poland), where demonstration was more rare, less detailed and supported by simple and short commands:

1   A partner approaches me [a partner approaches]
2   I push the partner [the coach pushes the partner away]
3   He comes again [the partner comes up again]
4   I drag the partner [the coach pulls him]
5   and I perform my technique [the coach throws the partner]

(VO, PL, judo4, M)

1   You have to pull back [the coach pulls back]
2   Shift [the coach shifts his hand]
3   [the coach moves to a hold without commenting on it]

(VO, PL, judo5, M)

In the most advanced judo group, the coach started using demonstration in the second part of the training session after making the statement 'Now we will work on our technique'. The participants of this group were the least interested in their coach's demonstration. One can suppose that in this case the participants had already quite well developed their 'theoretical knowledge how', and some of them their 'practical knowledge how', therefore it was less important for them to follow the coach's demonstration; in the other, less advanced groups, the learners were focused on the coaches' demonstration, thanks to which they learnt how to do a particular technique.

4.2.2.2   Athletics

Demonstration is also the main method of knowledge transfer in athletics, although the conducted observations show that it is used less often than in judo. The training sessions in this sport were much more diversified than the judo trainings, which resulted from the discipline itself, the learners' age and their sport experience. A part of the sessions, mainly in the case of the youngest groups, was focused on body conditioning exercises, while others were dedicated to a particular technical discipline, such as javelin, hurdles or pole vault. The coaches working with the smallest children and/or beginners showed each exercise, even during warm-ups. In the most advanced and/or older groups, demonstration was usually used during the main part of the training sessions when technical exercises with sports equipment were being practised. For examples, in both Poland and France, the coaches demonstrated the techniques for the javelin throw and the pole vault.

During the interviews the coaches stated that they did the demonstrations themselves or asked more experienced learners or athletes who were present in the stadium to show the correct technique of how to run, throw or jump. This way the learners have the possibility to observe the best athletes and to imitate their movements in the most exact possible way:

> They observe. They should watch the best and imitate him/her. Imitation. The method of imitation is the basis.
>
> (athletics, M2, SI)

Most of the observed demonstrations were made by the coach him/herself, although the coaches also asked one learner to demonstrate the correct way of performing an exercise and the others to watch him/her. During one Polish training session in athletics, the coach first asked the learners to observe a more advanced athlete who was training at the same stadium and then asked one of the girls to demonstrate to the others how to practise on the hurdles. During another athletics training session, also in Poland, the coach recommended that one girl observe how another girl was practising and try to imitate her movements.

Demonstration during training sessions in athletics was limited in several cases. First was when the training session's aim was to play and to provide physical activity rather than teach sports skills. Second, demonstration was more rare during training sessions with more experienced athletes, which had also been observed in judo. And, third, one could notice a considerable disparity between the ratio of utterances and demonstrations in running and technical exercises. This can be explained by some of the coaches' conviction that it is not possible to demonstrate how one should run ('a pure form' of running) because each athlete has to adapt the movements to his/her physiology and find his/her own way of running; however, this did not pertain to hurdles, since for this discipline the coaches used demonstration often to show the correct way of jumping over a hurdle. In this dimension, hurdles races are closer to the javelin or pole vault than to track races.

4.2.2.3   Swimming

In swimming, demonstration was used more frequently than in athletics, but slightly less often than in judo. The demonstration was always given only by the coaches themselves. The more advanced the group was, the less frequently demonstration was used. For example, in one training session, the only demonstration resulted from one learner's two-week absence and the necessity of having to repeat for him an exercise connected with the butterfly stroke. In the case of less advanced groups, demonstration was used before each new exercise, with the exception of warm-ups both in and outside the water.

The aspect that distinguishes this sports discipline is the possibility to demonstrate a movement in the water and outside the water. During the observed training sessions, it was always the second solution, but in the interviews, the coaches emphasised the advantages of both kinds of demonstration, which can be illustrated in the following statement:

> At the beginning, when starting teaching swimming, it is good to make a demonstration in the water. The main reason for this is to make the children feel safe and to guarantee safety and security. They sometimes ask – how is it possible that the coach teaches swimming but does not enter into the water. Demonstration in the water is a bad idea, because

the water narrows down the demonstration. One cannot see the movement precisely. And demonstration on dry land works much better. First, [one has to] describe something in short, name it, show the exercise's goal, and then make the demonstration on land. There one can demonstrate almost everything. And the coach sees much better. They see everybody and can keep each of the children posted as to what he/she should change.

(swimming, W2, SI)

However, as was noted by one of the female coaches, sometimes it is necessary to enter into the water:

Once I had such a situation in which I had tried to explain for a long time a flip turn, and they were not at all able to understand how they should do it, which movement, when, etc. It made me furious, so I put on my swimsuit, jumped into the water and demonstrated it to them. And then it was much better.

(swimming, W2, SI)

This coach returned to the issue when answering the question as to what is the most difficult to explain only through words. Teaching the breaststroke illustrates the difficulties of demonstration in swimming:

One does not know really how to demonstrate it. It is not totally visible in the water, while outside of the water the legs move completely differently than in the water. In the water, they should loosely fall during the movement, but how can one demonstrate it? It is very difficult.

(swimming, W2, SI)

Another female coach drew attention to the difference in children's behaviour when the coach is in the water and when he/she is outside the water:

When the children see that you are in the water, they swim worse. Yes, it has been proven. I once read research on it. The children know that they can allow themselves more, they can make jokes or something else because they know that we [the coaches] will swim up, catch them and help them. When the children see that we are outside the water, they are forced to rely on themselves only.

(swimming, W1, SI)

She also stated that even if it were better to make a demonstration in the water, to swim in front of the training session participants, staying in the water all day long is not healthy for the coaches, and for this reason she prefers to stay outside of the water:

> I could stay all the time in the water, because I know that it would be better, but physically we are not able to do it.
>
> (swimming, W1, SI)

The issue of demonstration in and outside the water also appeared during the apprenticeship. The field notes from the swimming sessions reveal just how important the 'natural' material environment is during teaching and learning sports skills. The short training sessions took place outside the water, and both the coaches and the researchers were sceptical about the possibility and sense of learning some swimming skills during a dry land workout:

> After finishing the interview, I asked the coach to teach me the basic movement of the hands in the crawl. The coach immediately stated that it is not possible to learn swimming during a dry land workout, first without the water, and second, without practising the movements as demonstrated by him, which is impossible without entering into the water.
>
> (AP, swimming, M2)

> For me, the most difficult was the dry land workout: to take an unnatural posture on dry land that imitates swimming and coordination of all these movements in the air.
>
> (AP, swimming, W2)

> Swimming on dry land is something abstract, mainly because I have never swum the crawl. (. . .) Similarly, the female coach did not see any sense in swimming outside the water. She demonstrated to me what I should do, however without any enthusiasm.
>
> (AP, swimming, W1)

The swimming example is distinct because the demonstrations were made only outside of the water, that is, outside the 'natural' environment of a swimmer's movement. The demonstration was usually focused on the movements of the hands and head as well as on breathing, and rarely on the leg movements. In relation to footwork, the coaches usually used short commands, such as 'legs crawl' or 'legs butterfly stroke'. When they demonstrated the leg motions, this was almost always done with the hands, not the legs; therefore, the coaches' demonstrations (done with another part of the body) did not reproduce precise movements but rather gave a general idea of the movement and/or served as a reminder that a movement should be performed correctly.

4.2.2.4 Making the demonstration more visible

The first ability that learners have to learn is 'to see what is being demonstrated' (Schindler 2009: 144). Schindler distinguished four coaching practices whose aim is to allow training session participants to see more: (1) reduction in speed – showing a movement in slow motion, (2) fragmentation – displaying a movement step-by-step, (3) repetition and (4) commentary –demonstrating and commenting on a movement at the same time (Schindler 2009: 146). All of these practices were observed during the training sessions in both Poland and France.

While displaying a movement, the coaches reduced the speed to make particular elements more visible. In judo, athletics and swimming, the demonstration was very often conducted in slow motion at the beginning of the 'teaching unit'. Then the speed was increased to the 'natural' speed used during a fight or athletics competition. In swimming, the pace of the different movement also partially resulted from the fact that the coaches did not display the movements in the water but outside of it.

The practice of reduction in speed had already been mentioned by the coaches during the interviews:

> First, I do this during a demonstration. At the beginning slowly, and then the movement at full speed.
>
> (athletics, M2, SI)

> I use it for throws. I demonstrate to them at a slow pace to let them see how the hand should move, what the trunk turn should look like. Then I use a faster pace.
>
> (athletics, W3, SI)

It was also observed during the apprenticeship:

> The coach knelt down and started to demonstrate. He showed very slowly all of the sequences of movements necessary to start and described, at the same time, what he was doing, in what way I should take on the body position, how to move on to the next phases to avoid mistakes. Afterwards, he showed me the correct movement at a speed close to the start's speed.
>
> (AP, athletics, M2)

Although a reduction in speed is commonly used and perceived as helpful, it can also be confusing to the learners, as was mentioned by one of the coaches:

> I noticed that when I make a demonstration at a slow pace to allow them [children] to understand it, they themselves practice it slowly. They even repeat the pace.
>
> (judo, M1, SI)

Therefore, a reduction in speed used during demonstration makes the movement more visible to the learners, but at the same time it does not reflect the movement entirely and it does not reproduce its dynamics and appropriate pace.

The second practice as distinguished by Schindler (2009), fragmentation, was also very common during the observed training sessions. The coaches split the movements into single elements and motions of a particular part of the body. As indicated by one of the judo coaches:

> When we teach the throws, we split each throw into small elements, and afterwards we demonstrate it as a whole movement.
>
> (judo, M1, SI)

The same method, as declared by the coaches, is used in swimming:

> Swimming is difficult to teach because there are a lot of elements. Sometimes motion coordination is a problem, how to add to one another, the particular movements, and execute them with adequate frequency. We teach it so that at the beginning we practice single elements, and then we join them together to obtain complete movement needed in a particular type of swimming style.
>
> (swimming, W2, SI)

This was confirmed both during the training session observations and during the apprenticeship:

> First, the coach showed me a technique that I should learn. Very slowly, precisely, he split the whole movement into single parts.
>
> (AP, judo, M2)

> The coach explained the technique to me and demonstrated the particular elements of the movement. She combined each displayed element with a verbal description.
>
> (AP, athletics, W1)

> And then he started the demonstration and explained everything verbally at the same time. During the demonstration, at the beginning, he split the whole exercise into sequences, and afterwards he presented the whole fluent movement.
>
> (AP, swimming, M1)

During the demonstration, the coaches paid close attention to the particular movement of, for example, a foot or hand, which can also be perceived as the practice of fragmentation. This part of the demonstration usually started with words such as 'look' or 'watch how' – for example, 'look how I turn my right leg' (VO, PL, judo1, W), 'watch where his head is' (VO, PL, judo2, M) or 'look, we lift this leg lightly' (VO, PL, athletics6, M) – which can be seen as 'verbal pointing' (Schindler 2009).

Another type of practice of fragmentation are exercises both without and with sports equipment. This was observed during the athletics training sessions when the young athletes were practising first only the hand movements; then they repeated these movements with a javelin, pole or ball (in the case of the small children). Although, as the coaches claimed, this allows one to learn step-by-step and to make the techniques more comprehensible, as with speed reduction, it can pose some difficulties to the learners:

> It is sometimes very hard to demonstrate a movement. It works great without a ball, everyone is performing very well, but when they have to throw they automatically put their hand behind their head.
>
> (athletics, W3, SI)

Taking into account the fact that tacit knowledge is problematic to transfer verbally, the coaches very often used demonstration and tried to make it as visible as possible. However, they were also aware that sometimes it is very difficult to demonstrate a movement precisely. As a consequence, the coaches attempted to find a compromise between the demonstration's visibility and the movement's fidelity. Practices such as speed reduction or fragmentation of movement allow one to see more and to acquire new skills progressively, but they may also contribute to the acquisition of incorrect motion habits.

Another practice used by coaches to allow the apprentices see more was the repetition of a demonstration. This took place after the first demonstration, when a particular movement or its part was repeated. In this case, as was mentioned above, the subsequent sequence repetitions were faster than the first sequence. The coaches also decided to repeat a demonstration after observing the learners' way of performing a particular exercise. After the demonstration that begins a part of the training session, as described by the coaches, the learners are asked to make several repetitions of a particular exercise or technique. This part of the training session is sometimes interrupted in the whole group or in a pair of practising young learners:

> A thousand times, I sometimes interrupt the training session to demonstrate something because I prefer that they do something correctly once than a thousand times without any sense.
>
> (judo, M1, SI)

> One has to approach them, give advice, control them all the time.
>
> (athletics, M2, SI)

It cannot be so that there is a task, and somebody repeats it all the time without being controlled, being corrected. It has to be an ongoing analysis of movement. One has to control all the time all of the mistakes that appear.

(swimming, M1, SI)

The repetition of a demonstration was also indicated as the main method to correct the apprentices' movements:

[I do it] through demonstration and repetition of a correct movement, by approaching the learners and correcting a leg, repetition and positioning.

(judo, W2, SI)

I show them, and once again I demonstrate something.

(swimming, W1, SI)

Although one female judo coach cited above stated that she did not correct the mistakes verbally, because 'it is very difficult to explain it verbally' (judo, W2, SI), other coaches did indeed use this kind of communication:

I try to say or demonstrate that something is wrong. For example, today the children were jumping, and after each jump I said separately to each child what should be changed, [such as] a leg higher, a longer step, run faster, rebound from one, not two legs, etc.

(athletics, M1, SI)

In the coaches' opinion it is important to interrupt an exercise immediately and correct the movement in order to not lead to the development of wrong habits:

I stop an exercise and show the mistakes a learner has made and what a correct movement should look like.

(swimming, W2, SI)

It does not work this way, that a learner swims, and I do some correction once a week. I do it immediately, and then he/she has to practise to the bitter end, because it [a wrong movement] will become a habit and he/she will swim this way.

(swimming, W1, SI)

If there is a mistake, one has to interrupt them all the time, mainly during the teaching, because if something becomes a habit it is much worse to teach it from the beginning. So one has to correct, draw attention to it and repeat it. Repeat, repeat all the time.

(athletics, W2, SI)

The coaches' statements in the interviews were confirmed during the observations. The exercises were interrupted to see the coach's demonstration once again, and then the learners were asked to continue the exercises in the correct way this time. During the repeated demonstrations, the coaches presented the whole exercise or technique, or only the motions of a particular body part. In judo, the coaches made the demonstration in front of the whole group, with or without an opponent, but also in front of a particular practising pair or with one person from that pair. Several coaches used a repeated demonstration to show the mistakes that the learners had made. During the athletics training sessions, this use of demonstration method was observed only once. In swimming it was used by two coaches. In the more advanced groups in swimming and in judo it took place when the young athletes were practising and the coaches indicated only the part of their body that was in the wrong position or that they moved the wrong way, but the coaches did not say a single word. In the case of swimming, this could have partially resulted from the limited possibilities of being able to hear the coach when practising in the water.

During the apprenticeship, the members of the research team also had the opportunity to see the coaches' demonstration a second time:

> Second attempt. I already know the initial phase of movement in this technique, and I repeat it. While performing the next phase, I still needed the coach's help. It did not work. The coach demonstrated the exercise once again – he threw a boy. Third attempt. The coach repeated all the time what I should do and how to do it in the best possible way.
>
> (AP, judo, M2)

> After making a throw on me, the coach proposed that I repeat this throw on her. During this attempt, she advised that I be focused on all of the aspects that she had emphasised, and she demonstrated once again what I should be doing, one after the other.
>
> (AP, judo, W2)

One difference that was noticed between the observed training sessions and the researchers' apprenticeship was the simultaneous demonstration of the coach and the apprentice's performance. This happened twice when the researchers were learning the swimming and athletics movement. In both cases, during the renewed demonstration:

> When describing the activities, the coach showed what they should look like all the time. At the same time, he looked at my body position and asked me to choose my stronger leg and to put my body in the appropriate position. It is worth adding that I tried to do all the activities together with the coach, passing through all the phases, one after another.
>
> (AP, athletics, M1)

The coach described very precisely what I should be doing and at the same time showed all of the movements and exercises. He also asked me to conduct them simultaneously with him. He paid much attention to the mistakes and automatically corrected them by saying what I should be doing.

(AP, swimming, M3)

The absence of this practice during the observed training sessions probably resulted from the number of learners. During the apprenticeship, there was the coach and only one apprentice, and during the training sessions, there was the coach and the whole group. Therefore, the demonstrations were made for all to see, and it would not have been possible for a coach to display a movement and then to follow each person performing it.

The last coaching practice as indicated by Schindler (2009: 146), commentary, which is a demonstration and a comment on the movement at the same time, dominated during the observed training sessions. To learn more about this way of knowledge transmission, it is useful to look closer at the relations between verbal (commentary) and non-verbal (demonstration) communication. The analysis of the data gathered during the video recordings revealed the details and different forms of this relation.

At the beginning, it is important to state that one can distinguish between a simple gesture and a more complex demonstration. The gesture is understood as a movement of the fingers and/or hands, which refers to a particular movement of a part of the body, such as the arms, legs or feet. It is a shortened version of the complete movement, which helps to avoid redundancy and accelerate the process of knowledge transmission. In its second meaning, the gesture is a symbol which is recognised in a particular culture, whereas a demonstration is understood as a 'complete movement', a detailed and realistic display of the exercise or its part.

On the basis of the conducted analysis, several relations between gestures or demonstrations and verbal utterances were revealed. First, one could observe that the coaches' movements appeared simultaneously along with words and exactly expressed what was being said, such as

We bend [the coach bends his/her legs] *legs.*

(judo)

I push [the coach pushes a partner] *a partner.*

(judo)

We run [the coach runs] *to the middle line.*

(athletics)

I turn [the coach turns].

(swimming)

This practice was observed mainly during explanation, when the coaches demonstrated a movement and at the same time commented on it. It was connected with fragmentation of demonstration.

Second, one could also observe the coaches' displayed gestures that appeared together with a word but did not (exactly) overlap with that word, such as

and the head [the coach points a finger up] *follows the hand*

(judo)

the pinky finger [the coach waves his/her hands]

(swimming)

In these cases, the words emphasised the part of the body that did not move in the correct way, and the displays demonstrated how this should be done; however their range was wider, as illustrated by the example of one finger and the whole movement of the hand. In other situations, the gestures indicated the direction of movement.

The coaches also added to the words particular gestures that are common worldwide (e.g. come here, numbers) or in Polish (sports) culture. An example from Poland can be Kozakiewicz's gesture, which is used in teaching judo.[1] This kind of gesture is very helpful during the teaching process, even if it is only verbalised, which was emphasised by one coach during the apprenticeship:

> During the first sequence [of movements], the coach told me that the best way to explain this movement to children is by using the expression 'show Kozakiewicz's gesture to your peer'. He said that when one tries to explain it in technical terms, the children do not grasp it. The expression 'show Kozakiewicz's gesture' activates them immediately and at the same time they perform the exercise'.
>
> (AP, judo, M1)

In the situations described above the utterances were quite clear, and the demonstration played a rather auxiliary role. In other situations, the role of the demonstration was the opposite, as display was crucial and was supported by verbal communication. This statement results from the analysis, which revealed numerous cases of using words that were not self-sufficient, such as 'here' or 'in this way'. The same can be said about the word 'hop!', which was used, as has already been mentioned, in multiple contexts. To make these utterances be understood, one has to demonstrate how the learner should move. This practice was very common, both in France and in Poland, and used in all of the disciplines. To emphasise the insufficiency of verbal communication, two versions of the transcription of several pieces of footage are presented, one without pointing to the moments and content of the demonstrations, and the other with them (Table 4.2).

Table 4.2 Role of demonstration in the verbalised transmission of tacit knowledge

Without demonstration	*With demonstration*
When you have a pole, you do it this way, when you grip the pole. Here, in front of you, when you grip, here. The hand goes here, close to the temple and up. Try. (VO, PL, athletics3, M)	When you have a pole, you do it **this way [the coaches takes the pole]**, when you grip the pole. **Here**, in front of you **[demonstration with the pole]**, when you grip, **here [the coach lifts his hand with the pole]**. The hand goes **here**, close to the temple and up **[the coach is holding the pole]**. Try. [the coach gives the pole back to the girl] (VO, PL, athletics3, M))
We grapple a judogi, that way, here. In the middle of the back, grapple the judogi, because we cannot grapple it this way. But we grapple it this way. (VO, PL, judo2, M)	We grapple a judogi, **that way, here [the coach grapples a partner's judogi]**. In the middle of the back, grapple the judogi, because we cannot grapple it **this way [the coach grapples it the wrong way]**. But we grapple it **this way [the coach repeats the first demonstration]**. (VO, PL, judo2, M)
(. . .) here, we have the arm stretched, the arm stretched upward, below the head. The arm is not here, the arm is below the head. OK? (VO, FR, athletics3, M)	(. . .) **[the coach takes a javelin] here [the coach demonstrates the arm position]**, we have the arm stretched, the arm stretched upward, below the head. The arm is **not here [the coach lowers the arm]**, the arm is below the head. OK? (VO, FR, athletics3, M)
The right hand all the time, you put it [in the water] all the time in this way and you should put it HERE and pull ahead. Once again. (VO, PL, swimming1, M)	**The right hand all the time [the coach demonstrates the hand's movement]**, you put it [in the water] all the time **in this way [the coach repeats the boy's movement]** and you should put it **HERE [the coach demonstrates the appropriate movement]** and pull ahead. Once again. (VO, PL, swimming1, M)
STOP, STOP. When you are here you stop. On the contrary, one should not stop here. Here, small and as far forward as possible. Without stopping here. Go on. (VO, FR, swimming1, W)	STOP, STOP. When you are **here [the coach demonstrates the hand movement]** you stop. On the contrary, one should not stop **here [the coach pulls the hands]**. **Here [the coach demonstrates the breaststroke hand movement]** and as far forward as possible **[the coach pulls the hands]**. Without stopping **here**. Go on. (VO, FR, swimming1)
I only draw back and hop. The legs go forward. (VO, PL, judo1, W)	I only draw back **[the coach draws back]** and hop **[the coach pulls a partner]**. The legs go forward. (VO, PL, judo1, W)
Dynamically, fast, and we turn to hold. HOP. (VO, PL judo2, M)	Dynamically, fast, and we turn to hold. **HOP [the coach throws a partner]** (VO, PL judo2, M)

The same practice was also observed by the researchers during the apprenticeship. One of them in his field notes wrote,

> Each demonstrated movement was signalised by the coach with the words 'and now this way', 'you catch him here', 'stand this way', 'legs here'.
>
> (AP, judo 1, W1)

The common use of words such as 'here' can be perceived as a kind of 'pointing gesture', as has been described by Goodwin (2003a). By pointing to a particular place on the body in his/her performance, the coach focused the learner's attention to this place. 'Here' will not be understood by learners if they do not follow the coach's demonstration. Additionally, pointing to something is in many situations more effective than precisely describing the place.

The gathered data revealed that the notion of 'commentary' is too narrow to describe the relations between verbal utterances and demonstration. Indeed these appear at the same time, but their roles and proportions are diversified. Sometimes the display plays a subsidiary role, while in many situations the comments would not be understandable without the display. Their proportions also depend on the sports discipline, age of the learners and particular exercise, which have already been partially described previously. One could also suppose that the differences result from personal differences among the coaches, but this interdependence has not been studied yet.

The common use of expressions such as 'here' or 'in this way' reveals that it is difficult to verbally explain the complexity of a given movement, although the gestures and displays can be perceived as an easier, faster and, what is particularly important, more effective way of communication. For example, instead of saying, 'you have to put your hand between' or 'I don't want you to move in the way that your right hand is', it is easier to demonstrate the correct movement.

4.2.3 *Visual tools*

The presentation of video films and other visual materials is treated, at least in Polish sports training manuals, as a kind of demonstration. However, none of the coaches described it as such and, in contrast to demonstration, it was nearly absent from the observed training sessions. This can be explained by the information provided by the coaches during the interviews, which stated that this method is used mainly during training sessions with senior athletes and/or those learners who take part in competitions:

> With the older competitors, yes, but with children the age I have, no.
>
> (judo, W1, SI)

It happens, but only with those children [who] have participated in competitions. I do this to show the recordings during the training sessions to make them see how they fought, what mistakes they made. But usually with children this age, I do not do it.

(judo, W2, SI)

When speaking about this method's usefulness, the judo coaches referred to their own experience and to the atmosphere during the competitions:

I know from my own experience as a sportswoman that even if you do something a million times, then you do not see it until you have seen it on a video recording.

(judo, W1, SI)

We very often record during the competitions. But, as everybody knows, during the competitions there are a lot of emotions. So it is easier to see the mistakes after the competitions (. . .) You have to analyse these mistakes, see where the mistakes were made, to make sure that the next time it is easier.

(judo, M3, SI)

In the case of athletics, two female coaches stated that they used recording as a training method, but in both cases only when they were working with older children (teenagers). One of them also mentioned that the athletes themselves recorded one another and analysed the recordings together.

The swimming coaches used video recording much more often and not only during the competitions. As they stated, today's technology offers the possibility to record training exercises and entire training sessions from different perspectives, including both above and under the water:

First, I record from the water, under the water. I can enter into the water with a waterproof smartphone and record a swimmer from above the water, and during each training session, I correct an athlete. It is very easy now. So I record the swimmers nearly during each training session. I record them and then I show it to them.

(swimming, M3, SI)

While some of the coaches show the recordings to each swimmer and discuss them with him/ her, one coach gathered the recordings and presented them to all of the learners by discussing each athlete's individual errors. During the interview, he emphasised the advantages of using this method:

I tell them to make use of all the lessons, to learn from the mistakes made by their peers in order to not repeat the same mistakes.

(swimming, M1, SI)

During the interviews the coaches were also asked when they usually used the visual method. The aim of this question was to find in which situation(s) video recording was perceived as a better and more effective teaching tool than verbal communication or when verbal explication was insufficient. Two main arguments were indicated by one of the judo coaches:

One the one hand, we use video recording to show how the best [athletes] are doing this. On the other hand, if you show their fight, we do this to indicate the mistakes. In this case, it is about learning, about enhancing their skills.

(judo, W1, SI)

With reference to the first argument, one swimming coach emphasised that they used films with the best swimmers when he wanted to 'present accuracy and professionalism of movement' (swimming, W2, IS). The best athletes demonstrate a 'pure form' (Hughson and Inglis 2002: 3) of sports movement and sports skills, and, as a consequence, their performances can be used as teaching tools (a pattern of excellence) and as inspiration and role models for the young athletes:

When I do not know how to demonstrate something or we refer to an example that is completely new and I do not plan to teach it or I am not able to teach it, it is better to use something that, for example, a world champion is doing – How are they doing this? How do they move? And then we use some examples from the competitions.

(swimming, M3, SI)

The visual method is something that I use very often. I use social media, instant messenger, and send children YouTube films with different competitions, [such as] world championships.

(swimming, M2, SI)

The use of YouTube fits into the wider trend related to the growing role of video-sharing websites, such as YouTube, in sports teaching and recreational sport (Quennerstedt 2013a, 2013b). However, it remains in the margins of this project. In contrast, it is important to notice that the coaches are aware of the limits of their possibilities of being able to demonstrate the most appropriate way of performing each movement and give their learners the possibility to imitate the best performances.

Coaches from all of the studied disciplines also stressed that video recording give the possibility to show the learners their mistakes. One of the coaches stated:

> As it is known, if a person does not see it, then they are not able to do it, when somebody does not show you that you have made a mistake. In the case of a kick, a run, a swim, where you're putting a hand incorrectly, you will not believe it until you see it [seeing is believing].
>
> (swimming, M1, SI)

This use of video was observed during one training session in swimming (VO, PL, swimming1, M). From the beginning of this session, the coach drew attention to one learner's hand movements and instructed him both through verbal comments and demonstrations. Despite the coach's remarks the boy still continued making the same mistakes. The coach decided to register his movements on a mobile phone and showed him his way of swimming. After seeing his mistakes and with additional explanation, the boy understood how he should be swimming, and the coach had no more remarks to make to this learner.

During the researchers' training sessions, only one coach (of swimming) used visual instructions to explain the movements:

> At the beginning, by using the visual materials that were at the swimming pool, the coach showed me a poster which presented the phases of swimming the crawl. He explained to me that taking a breath and a correct body position are important, as well as synchronisation of these two elements and, at the beginning, the hand position along the hips. During this verbal explanation of the poster's content, he demonstrated to me what this should look like.
>
> (AP, swimming, M2)

Although the use of the visual method was nearly absent during the observed training sessions, all of the coaches agreed that this method is very useful. The data gathered during the interviews allow the conclusion that the researchers' teams did not have the opportunity to notice them because of the age and sports level of the observed learners.

4.2.4   *Imaginative methods*

Although none of the coaches had listed imaginative methods when answering the open question about teaching methods, when asked about them directly, some of the coaches stated that they are more common among the adults than youth whereas other coaches (from judo and swimming) stated that they used some forms of imaginary exercises:

Sometimes we use comparisons during the training sessions with smaller children. For example, we make bubbles that look the same way when water is boiling, or we make it look like we're cooking a soup and the water is boiling. We also say that we're jumping into the water like small balls. But we do not say, 'and now think what it looks like', and they are sitting and thinking. No, no. We show it and compare it to something that they know, something from stories.

(swimming, W1, SI)

We imitate some movements. This is used mainly in a playful form. You can imitate different animals, different beings living in oceans or seas. The children have to be able to imagine this and try to imitate it.

(swimming, M1, SI)

In this context, the second coach cited here drew attention to a seemingly unimportant issue that can be omitted by adults:

First, one has to ask if the children know what it look likes. Because if a child does not know what, for example, a jellyfish, octopus or seal looks like, it is difficult to do. A child will not imagine this when they do not even know what it looks like.

(swimming, M1, SI)

The coach noticed that one has to be up-to-date with fairy tales and animated series in order to make references to their heroes and heroines. For example, when he teaches the breaststroke, which in everyday Polish is called the 'small frog', he asks the children to think about a frog that they know from some fairy tale. Yet another coach noticed that one has to be careful when using this method during the children's training sessions as regards their imaginative competences:

But with children it is difficult to use the imaginative method, because children are not able to imagine everything in the appropriate way. It also depends on their age and level. It can sometimes have a dangerous effect, for example when a child thinks that he is Superman.

(swimming, M2, SI)

In swimming, the imaginative method is usually accompanied by a demonstration; therefore, it rather has an auxiliary character. In judo, in turn, this method is more important, and it is used when trying to imagine an opponent:

In judo we use 'fight with a ghost'; that is, we imagine that a partner is standing in front of us, and we repeat some movement without that

partner, although still thinking that they are there. We repeat this twenty
or a hundred times. The aim is to develop an unconditional reflex.

(judo, W2, SI)

The most often observed imaginative method in all three disciplines was the
use of metaphors. A male swimming coach, when showing an arm movement, explained that children should imagine that there is a high wardrobe
or a shelf, and they want to reach for something that is on top: 'It is this
movement. You take something that is high, and the second hand also takes
something that is high' (VO, PL, swimming3, M). His explanation was supported by his arm movements, similar to the second use of metaphors, when
he compared an arm to an oar by emphasising that the whole arm is an oar,
not only the hand. A female swimming coach, in turn, explained the forward
roll in the water by using the metaphor of a small ball (VO, PL, swimming4,
W). A female athletics coach compared, for example, the arms to broken
wings and asked the children to run rather as butterflies than as elephants,
thus stressing that she did not want to hear anything (VO, PL, athletics5, W).

During the short training sessions with the members of the research team,
the coaches also used metaphors which were, as the field notes revealed,
helpful:

The coach explained to me some of the movements through comparison, for example, that we take the wheel.

(AP, judo, W2)

I have to admit that I had the least problems with the first sequence [of
movements]. The expression 'Kozakiewicz's gesture' allowed me to understand it correctly. Maybe without it I would have had more difficulties.

(AP, judo, M1)

The coach used comparisons when describing and showing the movements. For example, he said, 'put your head as if on a boyfriend's
shoulder'.

(AP, swimming, M3)

The meaning of metaphors in the transmission of either tacit or implicit
knowledge has been discussed by several authors. As George Lakoff and
Mark Johnson (1980) stated, 'the essence of metaphor is understanding and
experiencing one kind of thing in terms of another' (p. 5). From the point of
view of the research problem being analysed here, the most important fea-
ture of metaphors is the possibility of being able to express tacit knowledge,
as has been noted by different authors. According to Willard Van Orman
Quine, thanks to metaphors one is able to formulate what 'resists literal

communication' (1996: 160). In Paul Ricoeur's opinion, metaphors have the capacity to 'provide untranslatable information' (1996: 141), whereas Karsten Harries stated that 'metaphor transcends what can be captured by language' (1996: 72).

Karin S. Moser (2004) showed the role of metaphors in representing (transferring and acquiring) implicit knowledge with reference to 'work process knowledge' and knowledge management. She stated that the metaphor should be understood as one of the most important strategies used to represent complex and abstract concepts, which seems to be particularly important in sports skills acquisition. She also stressed that metaphors, understood as the creation of analogies, are crucial in acquiring new knowledge, as 'by forming analogies we can structure and understand new and unfamiliar knowledge along the lines of the familiar' (Moser 2004: 153).

Sylvia Faure (1999) emphasised the role of metaphors in finding the appropriate way to correctly perform a dance movement. She stated that metaphors can refer to both visual and kinetic sensations, which she illustrated by using a dinosaur's tail as an example, as thinking of having this tail should prevent children from lifting their buttocks. The use of metaphor as a tool of tacit knowledge transmission has been confirmed in the conducted study, mainly with reference to the youngest groups.

4.2.5 Proxemics

Proxemics (Hall 1966, 1968) is not distinguished as one of the main methods of knowledge transfer; however, it does appear as one form of non-verbal communication (beside paralinguistic and kinesics) in both Polish sports manuals (Czabański 1996; Wiesner 2005) and scientific publications (see, e.g. Castañer *et al.* 2013). The current study revealed that this form of communication should be analysed in two dimensions: first, as the distance between the coach and the whole group and space arrangement; second, as the distance between the coach and individual learner(s).

Both sports disciplines and training courses differentiate the use of space. During warms-up in judo, the coaches utilised all of the space in the gymnasium; the learners were running and did some exercises along the walls, or they were practising in two rows. In athletics, the warm-ups usually took place in the same place as the main part of the training session, although in single cases the coaches also used other places, such as a running track (when the learners had to complete two or more laps to warm up) or a pitch. In swimming, most often only the pool was used; however, in a few cases the first part of the warm-up was conducted outside the water.

As for the main training part, one could easily distinguish moments during which all of the training participants were (or at least should have been) focused on the coach and on his/her instructions (usually explanation with a demonstration) and those parts when they were practising. These were related to different space arrangements, which was also observed in another study on martial arts (Schindler 2009). When the coach introduced a new exercise, all of the participants were focused on him/her, sitting, kneeling or (more rarely) standing in front of the coach in a row, along two walls or around the coach. During the exercises, they practised on the whole mat, each occupying only a small piece of it – individually and in pairs. Alternatively, they practised in two rows, one by one, from one edge of the mat to the other. In the case of more numerous groups and small gymnasiums, during the exercises in pairs, the groups were divided into two to allow everybody to practise in a sufficiently large and safe space. During these activities, the coaches behaved in different ways, although two main common patterns could be distinguished. Some of the coaches would stand close to the wall and observe the group (although not all the time, as the GoPro cameras revealed), and from time to time they would intervene by approaching a practising person or pair to give their comments and recommendations or to directly correct the movement. Other coaches moved almost all the time among the learners and gave them different kinds of comments or 'hints'. In France, this second type of behaviour was more common, which could have resulted from the different types of coaching education, various 'schools of training' or cultural differences. This is one of the issues that requires further studies in terms of the global character of sport and multi-national club teams.

In athletics, it was difficult to distinguish one or two dominant behaviour patterns. This resulted mainly from the range of sports disciplines that were being observed: sprints, middle distance running, hurdles, pole vault, javelin throw and long jump. Additionally, the groups had a different number of learners, from three to seventeen persons, and the training sessions took place at stadiums and in gymnasiums. However, one could observe that during the running training sessions, the coach moved more rarely and stayed

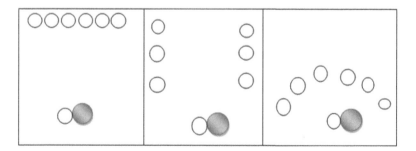

Figure 4.1 Space arrangement during demonstration (judo)

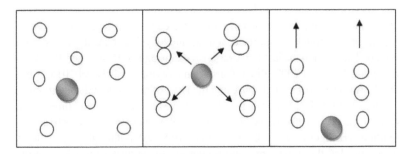

Figure 4.2 Space arrangement during practicing (judo)

in one place for most of the time, whereas during the javelin throw training sessions, the coaches moved together with the practising learners (they were walking in one direction, making one throw after the other). Similarly, during the pole vault training sessions, the coaches were quite active; however, due to the specifics of this discipline, the space on which they were moving was quite limited. The long jump, observed only once (in France), and hurdles, also observed only once (in Poland), should be situated between the running and technical disciplines. As for all of the observed athletics training sessions, it was not possible to distinguish the time for demonstration and that for practising solely on the basis of space arrangement.

In swimming, space arrangement is completely different, which results from the fact that the training participants are in the water (besides the warm-up that is conducted outside of the water) and the coaches are outside the water; therefore, with a few exceptions (e.g. learning the start from the starting block), there is no direct contact between the participants and the coaches. However, on the basis of the observations one can distinguish two main space orders. First, when the coach was presenting (explaining and/ or showing) a new task, the learners were gathered on one poolside and the coach was standing above them. Second, when the learners were practising, the coaches walked along the swimming pool to observe them and give some remarks. The video recordings revealed that the more advanced the group was, the less the coaches moved. An example can be found in one of the advanced French groups, in which the training session was focused on improving skills and its participants performed the tasks listed by the coach; as for their sports level, the coach did not have to observe the way they practised all the time.

The second dimension of proxemics is connected with the space relation between the coach and an individual learner. It is without a doubt that a part of the practices described above also concern individuals; however, one issue that is particular here is touch. In this case, the coaches passed the boundaries of personal distance and entered intimate space (Hall 1966).

The use of touch in sports coaching and physical education has been widely discussed in the last few years (Brackenridge 2001; Bringer, Brackenridge and Johnston 2002; Piper, Garratt and Taylor 2013; Burel 2014; Piper 2014). Awareness of sexual abuse and the issue of harassment during training sessions with children and young athletes have been raised many times. As a consequence, one can observe the trend to limit or avoid touch in coach–athlete relations (Bringer *et al.* 2002; Kerr *et al.* 2015: 56). Although some studies have revealed the importance and numerous advantages of touch in sports education (Kerr *et al.* 2015), it's perceived as 'fraught' issue (Piper 2014).

Therefore, one cannot be surprised that during the study conducted here this issue appeared during the interviews when the researchers asked about gender differences in sports coaching. Some coaches, when asked whether they worked with boys and girls in a similar way or whether they corrected their way of performing the exercises in the same way, started talking about the issue of touch. They were aware that touch can be perceived as something dubious and dangerous:

> Probably you are talking about touching, etc. I always try to not catch the children and not to shift an arm or a leg by force, etc. I prefer to say: left hand more broadly. I try to. For me, physical contact used to show a child what they are doing something wrong is an extremity.
>
> (athletics, M1, SI)

> In swimming, we enter with the children into the water. It is also a teaching element, but one has to remember that even if it is good, it might not always be perceived as good. And it is an issue one has to remember about.
>
> (swimming, M2, SI)

Another coach (of judo) did not speak about the 'touch problem', but he did draw attention to possible accusations of mobbing or sexual harassment:

> Nowadays one has to be careful about what one says to not be accused of harassment or mobbing, etc. In the past, a joke, such as when the coach said, 'watch out because we will knock out those teeth with those boobs', now there is no chance something like that will be said.
>
> (judo, M1, SI)

All of the cited quotations come from interviews with male coaches, which confirms the results from previous studies. They reveal that mainly male coaches are anxious about questions regarding the touching of young athletes (Miller, Franken and Kiefer 2007).

It should also be noted that the issue of touch was not raised by the judo coaches during the interviews. One can suppose that this results from this discipline's nature. Judo is a contact sport; therefore the touch of another person is crucial, whereas in swimming and athletics, sportsmen and sportswomen do not compete in a direct fight, but next to each other, or one after the other. Therefore, touch does not seem to be indispensable in their education and, as a consequence, the coaches might feel more concerned with the 'touch issue'.

Notwithstanding this concern that appeared in the interviews, the observations revealed that the use of touch is very common during the training sessions. The coaches very often crossed the boundary between personal and intimate space. One can say that using touch during a sports training session is something 'natural', perceived as an effective tool of tacit knowledge transmission. However, during interviews and when asked questions about touch, coaches start to think about touch and its social perception in a new, perhaps negative, way.

Touch was used in all three observed sports disciplines; however, in swimming, due to the nature of the sport, it was the least common. By touching the learners, the coaches corrected their way of performing a movement, adjusted some part of the body's position or helped the learners do an exercise. Moreover, the coaches also used touch during the researchers' apprenticeship. This teaching method was used slightly more often by the female coaches, regardless of the learner's gender. However, individual male coaches also used it to teach both female and male researchers. It should also be noted that two times in judo a throw was made with one of the learners, which could have resulted from the corporeal as well as skills disparity between the coach and the researcher. The coaches most probably assumed that it would be easier to perform the movement with one of the learners, although one cannot include awareness of the touch issue. According to the research investigators' field notes, most of the coaches felt comfortable and had no problems in correcting the body via touch:

> Seeing my body position, the coach came up closer and corrected my hands' position.
>
> (AP, athletics, W3)

> The contact was very easy-going. The coach freely corrected my movements, held me through my clothes. Physical contact was significant, identical as during a 'normal' training session and teaching of throws.
>
> (AP, judo, W2)

> First, the coach showed me and explained particular elements of this movement: the hand position, stretching out the hand with simultaneous

movement of the other hand, bending the hand in the elbow. Afterwards she put me in the right position (head and thorax). In the next step, she continued explaining the whole movement and at the same time led my one hand, correcting verbally or by touch the position of the second hand and my head.

(AP, swimming, W2)

The researchers found this technique useful, as illustrated by the following field note:

When I was doing this, he caught my hands and led them. For sure without his correction of my arms, my movement would not have been appropriate. At the same time, he told me what I should be doing.

(AP, swimming, M1)

Only in two cases (out of fifteen) were physical distance and embarrassment observed. One of the female investigators wrote:

The coach described and explained what I should do, what movements to make rather than showed something. You could feel a big distance from her. She did not correct me by moving my arms or legs. She corrected my mistakes by demonstrating the correct movements on herself.

(AP, judo, W1)

Cases of using touch to correct the learners' movements when the coaches positioned the body or its parts in the right way were numerous. For example, during the training sessions with girls practising the hurdles, the coach helped one learner who was having the most problems doing the exercises correctly several times. The camera registered, among others, the interaction shown in Figure 4.3a–f.

This footage illustrates a situation in which the coach does not explain the movement but rather forces the correct movement by changing the training participant's body position (e.g. legs or arms). The other athletics coaches, both Polish and French, whose training sessions were focused on the javelin and pole vault did from time to time change the positions of the learners' hands or even single fingers on the javelin and vault. In judo, correction by touch was very common, which results from the contact character of this sport. The coaches not only practised the exercises with the young athletes but also helped them to make a throw, a hold or, in the youngest groups, a roll on the ball. In swimming, the swimmers and their coach entered into an intimate space when practising the start from the blocks, which was observed both in Poland and in France. In Poland, besides this case, one

Come here....

And you do here...

put your leg here, closer to
the hurdle

.... and here. Why here?

and give the second leg

Here, high (VO, PL, athletics 3, M)

Figure 4.3 Using touch to correct the learners' movement

female coach used touch twice. In the first situation, the coach asked a girl to get out of the water, lie on the start block and demonstrated the movements she was doing in the water. Because the girl's movement was incorrect, the coach took her legs in her hands and started moving them in the correct way. In the second situation, the coach asked a girl who was in the water to give her hands and demonstrated with her hands how she should have been moving them.

On the basis of the interviews, one could suppose that awareness of the misrepresentation of touch between children and adults in contemporary society is one of the important barriers of embodied knowledge transfer. However, as the conducted observations revealed, touch is very often used as one of the most effective methods in the process of knowledge transmission. If one is not able to clearly explain how the movement should be performed, it is more effective to show on someone's body how he/she should do it or even force a correct movement by changing someone's body position.

Therefore, both the reduction in distance between the coach and the individual apprentice and the space arrangement should be perceived as important means of communication. Their main aims are to make a demonstration more visible to the whole group and to communicate knowledge that is difficult to transfer only with the use of words.

Note

1   This is a rude gesture (bras d'honneur) that Władysław Kozakiewicz, a pole vault jumper, made to a hostile crowd that booed, hissed and whistled during his performance at the 1980 Summer Olympic Games in Moscow after he broke the world record and won a gold medal. In Poland, this gesture became known as 'Kozakiewicz's gesture'.

References

Brackenridge, C.H., 2001, *Spoilsports: Understanding and Preventing Sexual Exploitation in Sport*, Routledge, London.

Bringer, J.D., Brackenridge, C.H. and Johnston, L.H., 2002, 'Defining appropriateness in coach-athlete relationships: The voice of coaches', *The Journal of Sexual Aggression*, 8(2), 83–98.

Burel, N., 2014, 'Du geste didactique au plaisir eudémonique. Le toucher de l'enseignant d'EPS, une communication des corps vivants' [From the didactic gesture to eudemonic pleasure: The touching of PE teacher, a communication of living bodies], in B. Andrieu, A. Paintendre and N. Burel (eds.), *Enseigner par son corps*, pp. 103–113, L'Harmattan, Paris.

Carlgren, I., 2007, 'The content of schooling – from knowledge and subject matter to knowledge formation and subject specific ways of knowing', in E. Forsberg (ed.),

Curriculum Theory Revisited, Studies in Educational Policy and Educational Philosophy, pp. 81–96, Uppsala University, Uppsala.

Castañer, M., Camerino, O., Anguera, M.T. and Jonsson, G.K., 2013, 'Kinesics and proxemics communication of expert and novice PE teachers', *Quality and Quantity*, 47(4), 1813–1829.

Collins, H.M., 2010, *Tacit and Explicit Knowledge*, University of Chicago Press, Chicago.

Czabański, B., 1996, 'Komunikacja dydaktyczna w procesie kształcenia fizycznego' [The didactic communication in the process of physical education], in B. Czabański and T. Koszczyc (eds.), *Dydaktyka Wychowania Fizycznego* [*The Didactic of Physical Education*], pp. 13–24, AWF, Wrocław.

Faure, S., 1999, 'Les processus d'incorporation et d'appropriation des savoir-faire du danseur' [The process of incorporation and appropriation of the dancer's knowhow], *Éducation et Sociétés: Revue internationale de sociologie de l'éducation*, 4(2), 75–90.

Gascoigne, N. and Thornton, T., 2013, *Tacit Knowledge*, Acumen, Durham.

Goffman, E., 1974, *Frame Analysis: An Essay on the Organization of Experience*, Harper and Row, New York.

Goodwin, Ch., 2003a, 'Pointing as situated practice', in K. Sotaro and N.J. Mahwah (eds.), *Pointing: Where Language, Culture and Cognition Meet*, pp. 217–241, Lawrence Erlbaum Associates, New Jersey.

Hall, E.T., 1966, *The Hidden Dimension*, Anchor Books, New York.

Hall, E.T., 1968, 'Proxemics', *Current Anthropology*, 9(2–3), 83–108.

Harries, K., 1996, 'Metaphor and transcendence', in S. Sacks (ed.), *On Metaphor*, pp. 71–88, University of Chicago Press, Chicago.

Hughson, J. and Inglis, D., 2002, 'Inside the beautiful game: Towards a Merleau-Pontian phenomenology of soccer play', *Journal of the Philosophy of Sport*, 29, 1–15.

Karpiński, R., 2001, *Pływanie: podstawy techniki. Nauczanie* [*Swimming: The Basics of the Technique: Teaching*], Ryszard Karpiński, Katowice.

Kerr, G.A., Stirling, A.E., Heron, A., MacPherson, E.A. and Banwell, J.M., 2015, 'The importance of touch in sport: Athletes' and coaches' reflections', *International Journal of Social Science Studies*, 3(4), 56–68.

Kuźmicki, S., 2011, *Judo. Historia i metodyka nauczania. Wybrane aspekty* [*Judo: The History and Teaching Methodology: The Selected Aspects*], Wydawnictwo AWF, Warszawa.

Lakoff, G. and Johnson, M., 1980, *Metaphors We Live By*, University of Chicago Press, Chicago.

Magill, R.A., 2011, *Motor Learning and Control: Concepts and Applications*, McGraw-Hill, New York.

Miller, M.J., Franken, M. and Kiefer, K., 2007, 'Exploring touch communication between coaches and athletes', *Indo-Pacific Journal of Phenomenology*, 7(2), 1–13.

Moser, K.S., 2004, 'The role of metaphors in acquiring and transmitting knowledge', in M. Fischer, N. Boreham and B. Nyham (eds.), *European Perspectives on Learning at Work: The Acquisition of Work Process Knowledge*, pp. 148–163, Office for Official Publications of the European Communities, Luxembourg.

Nyberg, G., 2014b, 'Exploring "knowings" in human movement: The practical knowledge of pole-vaulters', *European Physical Education Review*, 20(1), 72–89.

Orman Quine, W.V., 1996, 'A postscript on metaphor', in S. Sacks (ed.), *On Metaphor*, pp. 159–160, University of Chicago Press, Chicago.

Piper, H. (ed.), 2014, *Touch in Sports Coaching and Physical Education*, Fear, Risk and Moral Panic, Routledge, Abingdon, UK.

Piper, H., Garratt, D. and Taylor, B., 2013, 'Child abuse, child protection, and defensive "touch" in PE touching and sports coaching', *Sport, Education and Society*, 18, 583–598.

Quennerstedt, M., 2013a, 'PE on YouTube – investigating participation in physical education practice', *Physical Education and Sport Pedagogy*, 18(1), 42–59.

Quennerstedt, M., 2013b, 'Learning from YouTube', in L. Azzarito and D. Kirk (eds.), *Pedagogies, Physical Culture and Visual Methods*, pp. 162–177, Routledge, Abingdon, UK.

Ricoeur, P., 1996, 'The metaphorical process as cognition, imagination and feeling', in S. Sacks (ed.), *On Metaphor*, pp. 141–157, University of Chicago Press, Chicago.

Schindler, L., 2009, 'The production of <<vis-ability>>: An ethnographic video analysis of a martial arts class', in U. Kissmann (ed.), *Video Interaction Analysis: Methods and Methodology*, pp. 135–154, Peter Lang, Frankfurt am Main.

Schön, D.A., 1991, *The Reflective Practitioner: How Professionals Think in Action*, Basic Books, London.

Wiesner, W., 1999, *Nauczanie – uczenie się pływania* [*Teaching-Learning Swimming*], Wydawnictwo AWF, Wrocław.

Wiesner, W., 2005, *Komunikacja dydaktyczna na lekcjach wychowania fizycznego a poziom autorytaryzmu nauczycieli* [*The Didactic Communication during PE Lessons and the Level of Teachers' Authoritarianism*], Wydawnictwo AWF Wrocław, Wrocław.

5 Limits of tacit knowledge transmission and of its sociological exploration

Although some authors consider tacit knowledge as untellable and non-verbalised, this study confirmed that it can be partly transferred via verbal communication, which will usually be understood only in a particular situation or context (Gascoigne and Thornton 2013). The limits of its verbalisation can be considered in two different ways through the criterion of efficiency and possibility to transfer. The common use of demonstration and direct correction of the learners' bodies shows that utterances are not always sufficient or the most effective means of communication. Additionally, some elements of sports knowledge are perceived as nearly impossible to transfer, although they have their explicit definition. Examples of these will be described at the beginning of this chapter. In the second part, the main challenges related to the exploration and presentation of tacit knowledge will be discussed.

5.1 Unteachable – inexplicable

Skills, as was mentioned in the first chapter, can be learnt, mainly through direct interactions between the coach and the novice, and developed through practice. With reference to this definition, abilities can be understood as being different from skills. An ability is usually seen, as was mentioned in the first chapter, as the quality of being able to do something (Stanley and Williamson 2001; Snowdon 2003). However, it is also used to describe 'basic innate actions that underlie skilful performance' (McMorris 2004). In this second meaning, it is assumed that skills can be taught and learnt, while abilities are innate and can only be improved. With regard to this difference, it would be interesting to ask whether from the methodological point of view their transfer can be analysed in both cases and where the limits of its recognition are. To answer this question the examples of three abilities – a feel for the water, muscle memory and motion habits – were used.[1]

At the beginning of the research, the distinction between skills and abilities was not taken into account, and the differentiation between various elements of 'knowing how' was rather perceived in the possibility of their verbalisation. A feel for the water was perceived as difficult to verbalise and, as a consequence, difficult to explain; therefore, one of the questions addressed to the coaches was whether it was possible to teach it and, if yes, how they did this.

A feel for the water is one of the most important abilities in swimming. Its definition is presented in sports manuals, although in practice none of the coach uses this theoretical description. One of the coaches stated,

> What is a feel for the water? It is the water's taste, the water's smell, and so on [laughing]. It is described in specialist books, but without any basic practical knowledge, we are not able to describe it, and how can I demonstrate it to children? It would give nothing, a waste of time.
>
> (swimming, M2, SI)

Two female swimming coaches perceived a feel for the water as an ability, that is, as something that results from corporeal and physiological predispositions and as such is not possible to learn; however, they noted that there are some exercises one can do to improve it:

> R: Do you think that one is able to teach it?
> C: No. It depends on the body, on the bones. It is rather a physiological aspect, of body posture. (. . .) There are some exercises, but I think that it is time-consuming to teach it to somebody in practice.
>
> (swimming, W1, SI)

> It is not possible. A feel for the water is in the hands. One has to feel the water or not. Of course I can practise and improve it with good effect; there are different exercises. However, if somebody does not have a feel for the water at all, it will be difficult for him/her to swim well.
>
> (swimming, W2, SI)

In the opinions of other coaches, a feel for the water is possible to explain to some extent; however, it is mainly something that a swimmer has to 'feel' and experience on his/her own and requires practice:

> I am able to explain it to a swimmer, but they have to feel it. Unfortunately, I [can] not do this for them. But different competitors at different stages have this feel for the water, sooner or later. It does not work this way that at the same moment everybody should feel well in the water and have a feel for the water. One has to work on it. Work systematically.
>
> (swimming, M1, SI)

In athletics, but also in other sports, another one of the important abilities is 'muscle memory'. It has its definition in numerous manuals but, similar to a feel for the water, this definition is not used during the learning process. The question of whether it is possible to teach muscle memory and how one can do it came up as a problem for the coaches. All of them, instead of answering how they (could) teach it, talked about how one can learn it. This confirms that this element of sports knowledge should be perceived as an ability, as something that can be improved but is not transferred during interactions between the coach and the learner. One of the female coaches shared her experience of being an athlete and working on muscle memory and stated that she could not simply teach muscle memory. Another female coach simply answered that 'a lot of exercises' have to be done (athletics, W2, SI) to develop muscle memory. Two coaches emphasised the necessity of repetition, explanation and thinking:

> Through work, the hard work of repetition. A significant number of repetitions, often. We have to think during the training sessions, we have to think.
>
> (athletics, M1, SI)
>
> I think that it is possible to practise up to some moment. It should be based on demonstration and explanation. Explain, explain and demonstrate in slow motion, then a faster pace, the things that you were talking about.
>
> (athletics, W3, SI)

Only the second cited coach above mentioned the possibility of teaching 'muscle memory'.

The judo coaches were asked about another issue, namely 'motor habits'. Similar to the athletics coaches, they emphasised that this is something that is learnt rather than taught. The main tool of its acquisition is constant repetition:

> First, it should be repeated.
>
> (judo, M2, SI)
>
> In my opinion, through repetition, through repetition, possibly playing with the elements of this movement.
>
> (judo, W2, SI)
>
> It is the number of repetitions. I don't how to teach it; one has to learn it. Learn by the number of repetitions, strive to the stage where some things occur automatically.
>
> (judo M3, SI)

All sports knowledge is acquired by practice, numerous repetitions of a particular movement and experience. A part of this knowledge is communicated, mainly by demonstration and explanation, by the coaches, while some elements are nearly impossible to communicate. In this sense, abilities such as a feel for the water can be perceived as tacit knowledge as it was defined by Janik (1988), that is, knowledge acquired through repetition and practice, which is by its nature incapable of being *precisely* articulated.

This part of the knowledge can be analysed mainly from the point of view of the apprentice. An external observer might be able to see how this knowledge is used in practice; however, the process of its transmission remains nearly invisible. Direct interactions between the coach and the learner are limited in this case; for example, a novice cannot imitate a demonstration made by the coach. Therefore, although all sports knowledge is acquired by practice, in a majority of cases one can observe the process of its transfer based on communication (both verbal and non-verbal) between the coach and the learner. Being able to see the transmission of muscle memory, the feel for the water or motor habits is very difficult, if not impossible. From a methodological point of view, the borderline between skills and abilities can be seen as the boundary of sociological exploration. Abilities, described by Schön (1991) as *knowledge-in-action*, can be studied only by using such methods as autoethnography or participant observation, that is, via their *active* comprehension and bodily experience, so to the external researcher they will remain inaccessible. This inaccessibility in the field of sport is partly related to their inexplicable – tacit in the strong sense as defined by Adloff, Gerund and Kaldewey (2015) – nature.

5.2   Transformation of tacit knowledge into words

Some authors state that access to 'pure' tacit knowledge, a 'one-to-one representation of tacit knowledge', is not possible because it is transformed when it is translated into explicit (verbalised) knowledge (Adloff *et al.* 2015). According to Schön (1991), a researcher should be aware that a description of someone's knowing is a transformation of embodied knowing, which is to a large extent difficult to verbalise in an observer's words. He stated that a researcher who makes this description converts 'know*ing*-in-action to know*ledge*-in-action'. This issue has also been raised by Molander (1992), who drew attention to the fact that 'a description of something is normally not identical with what is described'. The interviews with the coaches, who were perceived as the experts, confirm that there is a significant difference between being able to do something or knowing how to do something and being able to explain how to do something. The explanation of sports knowledge and the process of its transmission remains problematic, as the limits of verbal communication were observed in many situations, both during the interviews and in the video-based observations.

The challenges related to expressing embodied knowledge were presented in the first chapter and in a few publications (Parviainen 2002; Crossley 2007; Samudra 2008). They were also noted by the project investigators who faced the task of converting their embodied experiences into words. As one of them wrote:

> Even now, when I am writing these notes and wondering how to put into words this experience, I am visualising in my memory the sequence of movements that I have learnt. I even take my hands away from the keyboard and repeat some of the gestures.
>
> (AP, judo, M2)

As this study reveals, the verbalisation of tacit knowledge is situation-dependent, not only during the training sessions but also during the situated interviews. As was mentioned earlier, in their interviews, the coaches very often used gestures and made demonstrations to visualise what they were talking about. In order to not lose the non-verbal data that appeared during the interviews, the researchers took notes of the coaches' demonstrations by trying to describe them with words in the best possible way. However, a better idea might be to make a video recording during the interviews, rather than only an audio recording. On the other side, this choice could discourage the coaches from participating in the research or could make them behave in an 'unnatural' way. Therefore, a researcher has to find a compromise between the possibility of seeing tacit knowledge and the research study's validity.

The second challenge related to the analysis of verbalised tacit knowledge is the numerous occurrences of words such as 'normal', 'appropriate', 'correct' or 'pattern movement', which can be illustrated in the following quotation:

> Everybody has some habits. Getting rid of them is the most difficult, as we want each pupil to perform a movement similar to **pattern movement**, to make the **correct** movement. Everybody comes in with some habits here. We have to teach the body position, **appropriate** rotation, **appropriate** motility, which is different from our motility in everyday life and in other sports.
>
> (judo, M2, SI)

In the case of these utterances, it is crucial to ask for an explanation and to pose questions regarding the things that are taken for granted by the sports coaches. This prolongs the interview but, at the same time, allows one to reveal the complexity of something that is obvious. Posing detailed questions and asking for extensive explanations leads to the emergence of facets of knowledge transmission that are tacit.

However, explaining what is 'appropriate' or 'correct' movement is also problematic for the coaches themselves, and for this reason they reach for demonstration or visual methods, such as video films. Knowledge that is transmitted through forms other than linguistic ones can be understood by the apprentices and acquired by them. However, in order to be analysed and shared with other researchers, it still has to be transferred into words. Audio and audiovisual material has to be in written form to 'make it accessible for the various stages of empirical analysis and publication' (Ayaß 2015: 507).

Transcription of video data remains a challenge for sociologists and other representatives of social sciences. This problem has been raised, among others, by Singh (2016b), who noticed that while one can speak about the strong impact of audiovisual data in qualitative research, sociologists still have to deal with the problem of the 'adequate representation' of audiovisual data in their publications and presentations during scientific seminars and conferences. Their representation should take into account verbal communication, non-verbal communication, the time of action and, in the case of sports studies, the spatial-physical movements of the athletes. The interactions seen on the video recordings should not be reduced to one kind of communication, as was stressed by Schindler (2009), but rather as a 'frame' (Goffman 1974) based on 'symbolic gestures' (Goodwin 2003b) which are

> built through the conjunction of quite different kinds of entities which are instantiated in diverse media: first, talk; second, gesture; and third, material and graphic structure in the environment.
>
> (p. 23)

In the literature reviews, one can find examples of visual data transcriptions (Goodwin 2000; Heath, Hindmarsh and Luff 2010; Luff and Heath 2015); however, in contrast to conversation analysis, one cannot speak of one standard, common pattern of transcription. Therefore, as Singh (2016b) stated, 'as long as there are no systematic procedures for visualising embodied actions in space and time, it appears more than reasonable to follow the "unique adequacy requirement"' (Garfinkel and Wieder 1992).

The problem of presenting the gathered data has been one of the most important challenges that the book's author faced. It results from a significant amount of research material and the limited book length, which forced a selection of data, as well as, and more important, the feeling that no form of transcription would adequately present the process of tacit knowledge transmission that is based to a large extent on non-verbal communication.

For this reason, different forms of data transcription were used to present the footage. The book's author is aware that these do not accurately or completely represent what was registered; therefore, one of the solutions to present better visual data would be to share with the readers the described footage (e.g. through a website). The solution would need to guarantee the participants' anonymity; thus, it would require some technological solutions and updates on ethical guidelines regulations.

Another problem that can limit the sociological exploration of knowledge is understanding knowledge itself: how it is defined and expressed in different languages (Harris 2007; Kresse and Marchand 2009). While in English the term 'knowledge' is used regardless of the type of knowledge, other languages make a distinction, such as *savoir* and *connaissance* in French. In the case of the study conducted here, the differences between French and Polish data were not revealed. This could partially have resulted from the limitation of the French study to only video-based observations, but also from the fact that the project's principal investigator worked on the data in a non-native tongue; she might not have been sufficiently attentive to some of the linguistic and paralinguistic tools. However, taking into account the tacit nature of the analysed knowledge, transmitted only in a small part verbally, the lack of any differences could also have resulted from the more universal nature of this knowledge transmission. They can be observed with reference to age, sports level and discipline rather than to culture and language. The issue of possible intercultural differences in the process of knowledge transmission has significant meaning when taking into account global mobility in sport and is worth further study.

Note

1 These kinds of abilities can also be found in other sports. Schön (1991: 55), for example, gave the example of having a 'feeling for the ball' in basketball, that is, the ability to repeat previous successful actions.

References

Adloff, F., Gerund, K. and Kaldewey, D. (eds.), 2015, *Revealing Tacit Knowledge: Embodiment and Explication*, Transcript Verlag, Bielefeld.
Ayaß, R., 2015, 'Doing data: The status of transcripts in Conversation Analysis', *Discourse Studies*, 17(5), 505–528.
Crossley, N., 2007, 'Researching embodiment by way of "body techniques"', *The Sociological Review*, 55(1), 80–94.
Garfinkel, H. and Wieder, L.D., 1992, 'Two incommensurable, asymmetrically alternate technologies of social analysis', in G. Watson and R.M. Seiler (eds.),

Text in Context: Studies in Ethnomethodology, pp. 175–206, SAGE Publications, Newbury Park.

Gascoigne, N. and Thornton, T., 2013, *Tacit Knowledge*, Acumen, Durham.

Goffman, E., 1974, *Frame Analysis: An Essay on the Organization of Experience*, Harper and Row, New York.

Goodwin, Ch., 2000, 'Practices of seeing: Visual analysis: An ethnomethodological approach', in T. van Leeuwen and C. Jewitt (eds.), *Handbook of Visual Analysis*, pp. 157–182, SAGE Publications, London.

Goodwin, Ch., 2003b, 'The Body in Action', in J. Coupland and R. Gwyn (eds.), *Discourse, the Body and Identity*, pp. 19–42, Palgrave Macmillian, London.

Harris, M. (ed.), 2007, *Ways of Knowing: Anthropological Approaches to Crafting Experience and Knowledge*, Berghahn, New York.

Heath, Ch., Hindmarsh, J. and Luff, P., 2010, *Video in Qualitative Research*, SAGE Publications Ltd., London.

Janik, A., 1988, 'Tacit knowledge, working life and scientific method', in B. Göranzon and I. Josefson (eds.), *Knowledge, Skill and Artificial Intelligence*, pp. 53–63, Springer-Verlag, London.

Kresse, K. and Marchand, T.H.J., 2009, 'Introduction: Knowing in practice', *Africa*, 79(1), 1–16.

Luff, P. and Heath, Ch., 2015, 'Transcribing embodied action', in D. Tannen, H.E. Hamilton and D. Schiffrin (eds.), *The Handbook of Discourse Analysis*, 2nd ed., pp. 367–390, John Wiley and Sons, Inc., Chichester.

McMorris, T., 2004, *Acquisition and Performance of Sports Skills*, John Wiley and Sons, Ltd., Chichester.

Molander, B., 1992, 'Tacit knowledge and silenced knowledge: Fundamental problems and controversies', in B. Göranzon and M. Florin (eds.), *Skill and Education: Reflection and Experience*, pp. 9–31, Springer-Verlag, London.

Parviainen, J., 2002, 'Bodily knowledge: Epistemological reflections on dance', *Dance Research Journal*, 34(1), 11–26.

Samudra, J., 2008, 'Memory in our body: Thick participation and the translation of kinesthetic experience', *American Ethnologist*, 35, 665–681.

Schindler, L., 2009, 'The production of <<vis-ability>>: An ethnographic video analysis of a martial arts class', in U. Kissmann (ed.), *Video Interaction Analysis: Methods and Methodology*, pp. 135–154, Peter Lang, Frankfurt am Main.

Schön, D.A., 1991, *The Reflective Practitioner: How Professionals Think in Action*, Basic Books, London.

Singh, A., 2016b, 'Timing and Acting – Reconsidering a Visual Transcription of Communicative Actions in the Case of Trampoline Training', ESA Midterm-Conference (RN Qualitative Methods) Qualitative Methods and Research Technologies, 1–3 September, Cracow, Poland.

Snowdon, P., 2003, 'Knowing how and knowing that: A distinction reconsidered', *Proceedings of the Aristotelian Society*, 104(1), 1–29.

Stanley, J. and Williamson, T., 2001, 'Knowing how', *The Journal of Philosophy*, 98(8), 411–444.

Conclusion

The study conducted here revealed that the concept of tacit knowledge is appropriate and fruitful when analysing skills transmission in the field of sport, and the skills themselves can be perceived as the embodiment of tacit knowledge:

> The sports activity has techniques and the sports teaching has procedure. The tacit knowledge existed in the sports skills. The sports body's mastering of sports technique is showed by the embodiment of its tacit knowledge in the sports skills.
>
> (Ma 2015)

Tacit knowledge in this area can be verbalised, although not completely; moreover, its verbalisation is situation-dependent. It is transmitted in the course of direct interactions between the coaches and the learners during the training sessions. The main teaching methods used by the coaches are demonstration and explanation. These very often occur together, although one can observe their different proportions and relations. Therefore, a detailed analysis of communication during sports training sessions should take into account the relation between language and other ways of communication. When words are insufficient or not effective to explain a movement, coaches reach for visual and imaginative methods. The former allow the coaches to present the best way of performing a particular technique; the latter are based mainly on metaphors, because children learn by making a reference to things they already know. Despite awareness of the 'touch issue', coaches very often directly correct the body's position; they help the learner to take the proper position or 'force' it by putting part or all of the learner's body in the appropriate place and way. Some aspects of sports knowledge should be perceived as tacit in the strong sense, that is, as being nearly impossible to articulate precisely. Moreover, a part of this knowledge and the process of its transmission remain invisible to an external, non-expert observer.

As has been mentioned before, no significant differences were found between sports knowledge transmission in Poland and in France. The four variables that to a large extent influence this process are age, sports discipline, sports level and type of exercise. In the case of the younger and, at the same time, less experienced groups, demonstration was more common. It was mainly observed in swimming, where in the most advanced groups the coach simply listed the tasks that were to be done. In judo, only in one group, the most advanced one, were the training sessions dominated by verbal commands, and one could observe a limited number of demonstrations, generally made by the learners themselves. In athletics, no significant differences were observed between the different age groups, but they were observed between particular exercises. In the case of the technical exercises, such as pole vault or javelin, demonstration was used much more often than in the case of running. Metaphors were more often used with the younger groups. In judo, imaginative methods were used, such as having the learners practise fighting with an imagined opponent. Visual methods, in turn, were more common during the training sessions with more experienced participants. The differences also depended on the phase of the training sessions, which could also be related to the level at which the learners knew a particular motion. The exercises that are practised during the warm-up are usually known; therefore, their demonstration is not necessary. They can also be perceived as less important in the learning process and in the acquisition of sports skills necessary to compete in a particular discipline. The distinction between 'theoretical knowledge how' and 'practical knowledge how', as proposed by Gascoigne and Thornton (2013), revealed itself as an effective tool to analyse the disparities between the use of different teaching methods and their relations and proportions.

This study has revealed that the transmission of tacit knowledge is visible to an external observer, mainly in the case of the younger groups, that is, the novices. When one start sports training, the coach has to, at least partially, make the 'knowledge how' explicit (Crossley 2007). It is also easier to see in contact sports and technical disciplines, while in swimming it often remains invisible. Training sessions for more experienced athletes are focused on skills improvement rather than on acquisition. As a consequence, this process is less accessible to be analysed, and the fewer interactions one can observe between the coach and the learners, the more difficult it is to see the process of knowledge transfer.

However, the issue of (in)visibility with reference to tacit knowledge should be considered in a larger perspective. One can refer to the notion of 'vis-ability' as used by Schindler (2009: 135), which is understood as the ability to see. In this wider context, tacit knowledge can be invisible at least for two reasons. The first reason is the issue of being an expert and/

or a learner of the analysed activity. The level of this familiarity influences the possibilities to 'see' what happens; therefore, one can ask if tacit knowledge can be explored by an 'outsider', that is, a researcher without any sports experience or who does not participate in the analysed practice. The second difficulty related to the 'invisibility' of tacit knowledge results from its nature, which pertained, to the largest extent, to the swimming training sessions. The participants, especially in the most advanced groups, were usually asked to do a defined number of laps in one style and afterwards to do it in a different way or to change the style. From the observer's point of view, these training sessions seem to be the least interesting because 'nothing happens'. One should realise, however, that this was also a process of tacit knowledge transmission was based on repetition and perpetuation of embodied habits. Therefore, tacit knowledge transmission is more difficult to 'see' in those sports that require long and monotonous effort, repetition of particular motions, and so on.

This kind of knowledge can still remain, at least to some extent, unrecognised in social science studies; for decades sociology has omitted tacit knowledge, despite its meaning in everyday life and in different social fields. Talk and text have dominated sociology, both in the theoretical and methodological dimension (Brown, Dilley and Marshall 2008). The growing interest in embodiment – the senses, emotions, habits and physical activity – has contributed to perceiving the body as both the site and subject of knowledge or of knowing, which is difficult to verbalise, and as such much more difficult to study. The appropriate methodology in the research of tacit knowledge still remains a challenge for both sociologists and other representatives of the social sciences.

References

Brown, K., Dilley, R. and Marshall, K., 2008, 'Using a head-mounted video camera to understand social worlds and experiences', *Sociological Research Online*, 13(6), DOI: 10.5153/sro.1818.

Crossley, N., 2007, 'Researching embodiment by way of "body techniques"', *The Sociological Review*, 55(1), 80–94.

Gascoigne, N. and Thornton, T., 2013, *Tacit Knowledge*, Acumen, Durham.

Ma, L., 2015, 'Analysis on Existence and Transmission of Tacit Knowledge in Sports Teaching', The International Conference on Education Technology and Economic Management, 14–15 March 2015, Beijing. Viewed 23 September 2016 from www.atlantis-press.com/php/pub.php?publication=icetem-15andframe=http%3A//www.atlantis-press.com/php/welcome.php%3Fpublication%3Dicetem-15

Schindler, L., 2009, 'The production of <<vis-ability>>: An ethnographic video analysis of a martial arts class', in U. Kissmann (ed.), *Video Interaction Analysis: Methods and Methodology*, pp. 135–154, Peter Lang, Frankfurt am Main.

Appendix A
The interview script

1 Introduction

1) How long have you been working as a coach?
2a) Who do you mainly train?
2b) Where do you train? [sports club, school, etc.]
3) Are you a coach only of athletics/judo/swimming?
4) Were you an athlete? What sport did you practise? Do you think that having been an athlete is necessary to be a good coach?

2 Teaching methods

1) What teaching methods do you use? [see the list if necessary]
2) Does their order matter?
3a) [if not mentioned] What type of methods based on demonstration do you use?
3b) What is the role of these methods?
4) As indicated by the manuals, one kind of teaching methods is based on imagination. How do you teach the imaginative methods?
5) Do you record the training sessions and/or competitions? If yes, do you analyse these recordings? In what way?

3 Non-/verbalisation

1a) Which activity/skill is the most difficult to explain?
1b) How do you cope with this? How do you teach it?
2) Please finish the following sentence:
    a) In words, the most difficult to explain is. . .
    b) I use visual materials when I. . . .
    c) Mistakes made by the learners I most often correct. . .

3) [swimming and athletics] In the manuals there is a lot of information about the appropriate angles of inclination of the arms, body, etc. How do you teach this? How can one teach an appropriate angle?

4)   [swimming] Is it possible, and if yes how, to teach a feel for the water?
[athletics] In athletics, one very often speaks of 'muscle memory'. Is it possible to teach it?
[judo] One stresses the meaning of motion habits. Is it possible to teach this?

4   Manuals

1a)   Do you use manuals?
1b)   Which manuals do you use?
2)   What is the role of drawings/photographs in the manuals? [show photocopies]
3)   What determines the way of visualising a particular exercise?

5   Gender

1)   In all of the analysed manuals, the drawings and photographs nearly always present boys and men. Why?
2)   Should boys and girls perform a particular movement in the same way?
3)   If not, do you have different visual materials for them?
4)   Do you perceive any differences in knowledge transfer (through different methods) between boys and girls?
5)   If yes, what determines these differences?
6)   Does the correction of mistakes look the same way for boys and for girls?
7)   Does a coach's gender matter in teaching?

Appendix B

Field notes from the video-based observations – guidelines

The field notes should start with basic data: date of observation, time of observation, place of observation, observed discipline, number of children, gender division, children's age.

Subsequently, the course of the training session should be described in a detailed manner. Attention should be paid in particular to

*   individual or collective performance of the exercises
*   gender division during the training session
*   methods of teaching (demonstration, explanation, etc.)
*   proportion between verbal and non-verbal communication
*   way an exercise is demonstrated (whole exercise, segmentation, etc.)
*   auxiliary materials
*   correction of movement
*   differences in behaviour towards girls and boys

Additionally, the field notes should contain information on the use of sports equipment and the use of space.

Index

Note: Page numbers in *italics* indicate figures or tables.

Taylor & Francis eBooks

Helping you to choose the right eBooks for your Library

Add Routledge titles to your library's digital collection today. Taylor and Francis ebooks contains over 50,000 titles in the Humanities, Social Sciences, Behavioural Sciences, Built Environment and Law.

Choose from a range of subject packages or create your own!

Benefits for you

» Free MARC records
» COUNTER-compliant usage statistics
» Flexible purchase and pricing options
» All titles DRM-free.

Benefits for your user

» Off-site, anytime access via Athens or referring URL
» Print or copy pages or chapters
» Full content search
» Bookmark, highlight and annotate text
» Access to thousands of pages of quality research at the click of a button.

REQUEST YOUR **FREE** INSTITUTIONAL TRIAL TODAY

Free Trials Available
We offer free trials to qualifying academic, corporate and government customers.

eCollections – Choose from over 30 subject eCollections, including:

Archaeology	Language Learning
Architecture	Law
Asian Studies	Literature
Business & Management	Media & Communication
Classical Studies	Middle East Studies
Construction	Music
Creative & Media Arts	Philosophy
Criminology & Criminal Justice	Planning
Economics	Politics
Education	Psychology & Mental Health
Energy	Religion
Engineering	Security
English Language & Linguistics	Social Work
Environment & Sustainability	Sociology
Geography	Sport
Health Studies	Theatre & Performance
History	Tourism, Hospitality & Events

For more information, pricing enquiries or to order a free trial, please contact your local sales team:
www.tandfebooks.com/page/sales

Routledge
Taylor & Francis Group

The home of
Routledge books

www.tandfebooks.com

For Product Safety Concerns and Information please contact our
EU representative GPSR@taylorandfrancis.com
Taylor & Francis Verlag GmbH, Kaufingerstraße 24, 80331 München, Germany